PRAYER-GIVEN
LIFE

THE PRAYER-GIVEN LIFE

EDWARD STONE GLEASON

CHURCH PUBLISHING
an imprint of
Church Publishing Incorporated, New York

Cover design by Stefan Killen

Gleason, Edward Stone, 1933 –
    The prayer-given life / Edward Stone Gleason.
        p.   cm.
    ISBN 978-0-89869-568-7 (pbk.)
    1. Prayer – Christianity. 2. Spiritual life – Christianity.   I. Title.
BV210.3.G56 2007
248.3′2 – dc22

                                                        2007016835

Church Publishing Incorporated
445 Fifth Avenue
New York, NY 10016
www.churchpublishing.org

5 4 3 2 1

THIS BOOK IS DEDICATED TO
ALL THOSE PEOPLE
WHO TAUGHT ME TO PRAY,
ESPECIALLY
CHARLES PHILIP PRICE
(1920–1999).
CHARLIE'S ETERNAL LIFE EMBODIES
THE DAILY PRESENCE OF JESUS CHRIST.

Almighty God, the fountain of all wisdom, you know our necessities before we ask and our ignorance in asking: Have compassion on our weakness, and mercifully give us those things which for our unworthiness we dare not, and for our blindness we cannot ask; through the worthiness of your Son Jesus Christ our Lord, who lives and reigns with you and the Holy Spirit, one God, now and for ever. Amen.

The Book of Common Prayer, page 231

CONTENTS

PREFACE

The Prayer-Given Life is rooted in my life experience and focuses on those parts of The Book of Common Prayer that have the most meaning for me. Evening Prayer and Compline, for instance, are not included, for although I know them well, they have not been central to my personal life of prayer.

Following The Book of Common Prayer, *The Prayer-Given Life* begins with twelve Opening Sentences from Morning Prayer and Evening Prayer, the tone of these lines setting the context for prayer. It proceeds to the General Confession from Morning Prayer that establishes our relationship to God and makes prayer possible. This is followed by collects that help us greet the day in prayer and lead on to passages suitable for private prayer, taken from the Holy Eucharist. The Eucharist is a corporate act, but since prayer is the practice of the presence of God, God's presence that comes to us in the Eucharist continues to be part of our daily lives in all moments, hours, and days that follow it. *The Prayer-Given Life* concludes with reflections on selected prayers and thanksgivings.

Our life of private prayer is a whole, but we enter into prayer at different points. The goal of prayer is always the same — the practice of the presence of God — but the avenues and venues differ. So you may read *The Prayer-Given Life* in sequence, just as it is written, from beginning to end, or you may drop in and out of a single chapter or one prayer within that chapter. This will depend on your mood, the time of the day, your hope for the practice of prayer at the time. In each moment each of us is unique, like no other person who has ever been or will ever be. So too, the time, one individual moment in the presence of God, will never come again in the same, precise way.

Millions upon millions of people throughout the ages have tried to enter the presence of God in the hope of prayer. The Book of Common Prayer spreads before us the words and lives of those who have gone before us, bidding us join them to be strengthened and uplifted by their experience of prayer.

My thanks to Deacon Kenneth Arnold, sometime Publisher of Church Publishing, who encouraged me to write this book, and to close friends and family members for permitting me to use their poetry: Anne Vermillion Gleason, Eliza Fernald Gleason, Charles Woolsey Pratt, Charles Blayney Colmore III, and to Morgan K. Smith Jr. for permission to quote his reflection previously published by Forward Movement Publications.

EDWARD STONE GLEASON
Eastertide 2007
Washington, DC

Prologue

YOU ARE MINE

Shortly before my fourth birthday, early one afternoon I walked upstairs for a nap in my small bedroom at the top of the stairs. Springtime, the month of May, clear and sunny, lying on the top of my bed, covered by a single blanket, I was completely alone, except for my Teddy Bear to whom I told all my secrets. The window was open, the curtains were drawn and flapping in the breeze.

Fully lit by strong, filtered sunlight, the walls were pale yellow, with glossy white woodwork trim that still smelled of fresh paint. Wide awake, I began to talk to myself. Conversation consisted of a single question, "Who am I?"

I asked the question aloud, "Who am I?" There was no answer. I asked the question again. "Who am I?" Still, no answer.

Looking up at the ceiling and its single light fixture, I repeated the same question, over and over and over again. "Who am I?" "Who am I?" "Who am I?" At that moment, an amazing thing happened.

The question became objective, as if asked from above, outside, beyond my own body. I saw myself from the vantage of the light fixture, stretched out on the bed. "Who am I?" "Who am I?" "Who am I?"

From this perspective, there was an answer — clear, strong, authoritative. "You are mine."

That experience never recurred, but the assurance remains. I am God's.

That moment marked the beginning of my life of prayer and provided a definition of prayer. Prayer is the presence of God.

Prayer happens in countless ways for vast numbers of people. It happens through words known and well-remembered and in words too easily forgotten. It happens in silence, during the challenge of exercise, vigorous debate and conflict. Prayer happens while we are sleeping. It surely happens in words that appear, unsummoned, on the spur of the moment, and through utterances that are wordless.

Prayer, no matter where and how and by whom it is expressed, is universal. We live in a world and universe where we are never alone. There is more. Some call what is more God, but named or unnamed, this context surrounds and defines us. Our life in its midst is prayer. Some who pray are Christian, others Muslim, Hindu, Jewish, Buddhist, or from another religious persuasion. Some claim no known or acknowledged manifestation of the divine; still they pray, whether they know it or not. They speak of a "higher power" or give such power no name; nonetheless, they pray. There are no atheists in foxholes; all people pray, some time, some how, perhaps often.

The fact remains, however, that we hear almost nothing of the universal practice of prayer. Why? It is because nothing is more personal than prayer. Every other intimate concern of human life has been dethroned, made comfortable for common conversation. Prayer remains sacrosanct, reserved for the innermost recesses of private life.

Young naval officers once were taught that three topics were never to be discussed in the wardroom: sex, politics and religion. Conversation today often revolves around these topics. The discussions that took place in my parents' living room and dining room avoided all mention of money or sex. It was unheard of to enter a house and ask, "So what did you pay for this place?" Real estate prices and sexual intimacies are now part of common parlance.

This is not so for prayer. Do you remember any recent conversation with friends or acquaintances that concerned prayer? It is rare. Even a monk seldom engages in the discussion of prayer in a social setting. Prayer is more intimate than sex or money or religion, more private than any other human concern. Prayer is at the very center of your being. Prayer defines the heart of our identity. Prayer is not a matter we choose to discuss. We would rather keep the matter completely to ourselves.

There are significant exceptions to the accustomed privacy of prayer. This book is rooted in such an exception that has opened new windows for understanding prayer in the lives of thousands of people.

For ten years I served as editor and director of Forward Movement Publications, whose mission is to support people in their lives of prayer and faith. It was my good fortune to spend several hours every working day in conversation, through telephone, e-mail, and letter, with hundreds of people who wanted to discuss what it meant to be a person of prayer. This was my rare privilege. Did these people have such conversations with a priest or pastor, a lover or spouse, a child or parent? This was unclear, but I doubted if these new friends, readers, clients, and customers spoke with another human being about what was absolutely central in their life: prayer.

They listened to God. They spoke with God. God listened to them. God engaged them. This led to an unusual opportunity: they welcomed me into the conversation that was their life of prayer. This was a new experience for me and for them, a window into the greater reality that all people are bound together with one another and with God through prayer.

Most of the people I interacted with were Episcopalians, and so conversation about their lives of prayer often related to The Book of Common Prayer (BCP). These conversations made me realize that I was charged with drawing others into this prayer book's rhythms, insights and patterns. In these conversations no prayer was mentioned more frequently than The Collect for Purity at the beginning of the Holy Eucharist:

Almighty God, unto whom all hearts are open, all desires known, and from whom no secrets are hid: Cleanse the thoughts of our hearts by the inspiration of thy

Holy Spirit, that we may perfectly love thee, and worthily magnify thy holy Name; through Jesus Christ our Lord. Amen. (BCP, 323)

This prayer sets the tone for private prayer with the realization that when God is particularly present, there are no secrets. This is one place and time when we are fully the persons God made and with whom God continues to dwell. As our lives open and respond to God's presence in prayer, we know the power of complete intimacy.

My life with The Book of Common Prayer Book began when our family knelt, usually for Morning Prayer, together in the pew on most Sunday mornings. Family life had two clear centers. The dinner table was one; corporate worship was another. The two were inter-connected. Table conversation concerned matters of importance: language, history, values, beliefs. The Book of Common Prayer was the source of coherence.

My parents were typical of many in their World War II generation. They believed in the privacy and primacy of prayer. Once seated around the dinner table, however, we revealed what was most important. What was believed important by those assembled bound us together as a family. Dinner table conversation revealed the considerable amount of time my mother spent on retreats sponsored by the Sisters of St. Margaret — retreats centered in The Book of Common Prayer. My father was far more taciturn, but at the dinner table I discovered that those persons whom he most admired and of whom he spoke most frequently were men whose lives were rooted in prayer. These were the people whom he held up to me as models and mentors.

It was inevitable that my confirmation experience would be memorable. More than a dozen seventh graders met on sequential Sunday evenings with the rector in his enormous office. Our Sunday school class that year was studying The Book of Common Prayer and preparing for our confirmation.

Our Sunday school teacher, Mr. Carr, was more than six-and-a-half feet tall, imposing and impressive, who stood at the end of the table at which we all sat. He had a black moustache, wore a gray suit, and spoke loudly and clearly. He and his wife were now childless, their only son killed early in World War II. He didn't need to say it, for we all understood that we had become his children, his family. The class did his bidding and occasionally met together for a party in the Carrs' house.

The curriculum in Mr. Carr's class was The Book of Common Prayer. Our task, as students, was not just to read, mark, learn, and inwardly digest, but to memorize. We memorized The General Confession in Morning Prayer, The General Confession in the Holy Communion, the Apostles' Creed, the Nicene Creed, and The General Thanksgiving. These assignments were not casual. In class after class after class, each of us stood, alone, and in turn, and recited what we had memorized. It did not take long before our recitations were close to perfect.

Although many of my professional years have been spent teaching secondary school students, I never followed

Mr. Carr's model. It was so old-fashioned, so pedantic and authoritarian. The fact is, however, that it worked. My understanding of the commitment one made in confirmation was immutable. The endless debate that a child at the age of thirteen is too young for adult commitment makes no sense to me. This was not my experience.

What happened in that year-long process and in the moment that Henry Knox Sherrill placed his hands on my head and said, "Defend, O Lord, this thy child with thy heavenly grace; that he may continue thine forever..." was a watershed. I was changed. The entire experience was marked by the words of The Book of Common Prayer. I learned that words from the Prayer Book mattered; they were pathways to a deeper understanding of the presence of God.

In *The Prayer-Given Life* I invite you to open your life to prayer, to be shaped and motivated by powerful private prayer. Each of us prays using words of our own choosing. The Book of Common Prayer offers words from insights inspired by countless lives of prayer. For nearly five hundred years The Book of Common Prayer has been created by the work of hundreds of people, and through repeated revision the Prayer Book has created forms and patterns to touch and guide your life in prayer.

Prayer is the place where human life opens to the presence of God. More often than not, prayer catches us unaware. *The Prayer-Given Life* suggests opportunities for daily prayer made possible by The Book of Common

Prayer, opportunities that occur when we allow its words to enter our lives.

You and I are changed when another person touches us, opens us, allows us to see that we are not alone, never alone. This happened once and for all time in the event we celebrate at Christmas, when Jesus Christ came into the world. Jesus continues to enter our lives through other persons, through the apostles' teaching and fellowship, the breaking of bread, and through prayer. *The Prayer-Given Life* opens the way for an experience of prayer known to countless persons who have gone before us and been grasped by the presence of God.

Chapter One

KEEP SILENCE

The Book of Common Prayer begins with the Daily Offices of Morning and Evening Prayer to mark the beginning and conclusion of the day. Each service is announced by an opening sentence, a brief statement to greet the beginning or ending of the day, to mark the season, and set a tone for each person who prays, day by day.

These opening sentences — brief statements gathered from well-known biblical sources — establish the framework for prayer. They are essential to the possibilities and promises that begin to unfold in the mornings and evenings of our lives.

> *This is the day which the Lord hath made;*
> *we will rejoice and be glad in it.*
>
> Psalm 118:24 (BCP, 39)

The only moment that truly exists is right now. It is all we have, all we know. The past is gone; the future is only a hope. What matters is right now. Pay attention. Let nothing escape notice.

This is the moment in which God is present.

It happened at 11:30 p.m. on a September evening, as we turned into the driveway. My wife, Anne, wrote this poem to capture the moment.

> Sitting in the corner of the garden.
> She is statue still.
>
> Our headlights catch the reflection of the
> Screech owl's eyes —
> Yellow-brown marbles.
>
> No movement.
>
> We freeze caught in the moment
> Of surprise.
>
> Mystery surrounds us.
>
> Pay attention.

The event she writes of, a series of moments, has become a "now" so crystal-clear that it is ours forever. What makes this true? Was it the event itself? The fact that we stopped and watched? Or was it Anne's poem? It is all of that and more. It was the surrounding silence that invaded and controlled us. We were in the presence of an Other, enveloped by awe and the awareness that we were welcomed into the world God made. God was present, and we knew it.

This is the world in which we live all day, every day. Too seldom do we stop and pay attention. When we do, God is present.

The Lord is in his holy temple; let all the earth keep silence before him.   Habakkuk 2:20 (BCP, 40)

God is present in the silence.

THE FIRST SUMMER of my two-year duty as a young naval officer was spent in Foxe Basin, north of Hudson Bay in the eastern part of the Canadian Northwest Territories. Our ship had been sent to help supply and construct the DEW (Defense Early Warning) Line, being built to warn the United States of a missile attack from the Soviet Union.

On a Tuesday, not long after we had crossed the Arctic Circle, heading north, just as I walked into the wardroom to sit down for lunch, the executive officer appeared at my side and said, "Mr. Gleason, the captain would like to see you in his cabin." Scared to death, I walked from the wardroom to stand before the curtain that opened into the captain's cabin and knocked on the door jam. The captain said, "Come in."

Sitting at a round table covered with a green felt cloth, he looked up and without asking me to sit down, said, "Mr. Gleason, I have just learned that you majored in geology. I'd like you to collect some geological samples from this area, identify them, and I shall send to the Navy Hydrographic Office for comment.

The executive officer has ordered a launch with a crew of three for your use for the afternoon. It is waiting at the gangway. Collect any tools you may need, dress warmly, go ashore, and report to me when you return. That will be all. Thank you." I saluted, turned to leave and do as I had been ordered, still frightened.

The three seamen in the boat were as green and bemused as I. No one spoke as we left the ship's side, until finally the boy at the helm asked, "Where to, sir?" I gestured toward the shore in the direction of a collection of rocks of all sizes, marked by several large boulders. The boat nudged slowly next to a large flat piece of glacial residue, and I stepped ashore, none too gracefully.

"Lay off a hundred yards or so," I said. "Keep an eye out, and I'll wave when I'm ready. It'll be two hours, at least." I turned and began to climb the steep slope ahead of me with no idea what to do next.

After I'd gone two hundred yards, I turned and looked back. The ship, riding at anchor, seemed far away. I turned to walk some more. Here and there, stone cover gave way to what I thought was mossy tundra. Before long it occurred to me that I'd better do what I'd been sent to do. I stopped to chip several samples with my hammer, designed for removing paint and rust from the ship's hull. The samples went into the pail I had brought with me. Pail, samples and hammer were set atop a large boulder to await my return. Then I continued to walk, up, up the hill, until the terrain began to flatten out.

When I turned to look back once again, the ship was even less visible, now seemingly in another world. I was alone. I could scarcely make out the thirty-eight foot LCVP that had brought me from ship to shore. The world from which I had come was unreal, toy-like. Only I was real, and now totally alone.

Or was I? Actually, I was surrounded by silence — complete and absolute silence. Everywhere there was silence, palpable, real, enveloping. There was not a sound, not a single sound. There were no voices, no distant whir of machinery, no sounds from the water, or the noise of the wind. Since there were no trees, there was no way to hear the wind.

This did not mean, however, that there was nothing. There was something, something amazing, wonderful and life-changing. I was enveloped, encased, surrounded, and uplifted, as I had never been by silence, complete and absolute. I had never been in such silence. It was overwhelming.

Through no action, no intention of my own, I knew I was in a holy place. I found a way to lie down, flat on the ground, my head on a small rise. There I remained, as still as possible, to look up into the gray sky and listen, just listen to the sound of silence, something I had never before heard. Time lost all meaning, and as it did, I knew what I was hearing was the voice of God.

God is present in the silence.

Watch, for you do not know when the master of the house will come, in the evening, or at midnight, or at cockcrow, or in the morning, lest he come suddenly and find you asleep. Mark 13:35, 36 (BCP, 75)

God, whom we may know only in part, is always ready to enter our life. Advent, the weeks before Christmas, asks us to make particular preparation for God's arrival, to open our lives in a special and timely way, right now, in this very hour.

This opportunity comes every day. The invitation that will make it happen — to open our lives to God's advent — is always ours. All-powerful and always present, God will never intrude, unless we desire it. We must offer the invitation. Any time, any hour of any day, will do. The choice is always ours.

The possibility remains that God will one day arrive with force in the fullness of time. How do we prepare for that moment?

An old friend, who would not consider himself a part of any worshiping body, wrote a poem for Christmas that described his Advent this way.

When the tsunami draws back its fistful of waters
And crushes the city, let me for once be ready.
Let me be washing the dishes or patting the dog.

When the great windstorm angles across the flatlands
Hungry and howling, let me be patting the dog.
Let me be kneading the bread or picking an apple.

When the ground shudders and splits and all walls
    fall,
Let me be writing a letter or kneading the bread.
Let me be holding my lover, watching the sunrise.

When the suicide bomber squeezes the trigger
And fierce the flames spurt and wild the body parts
    fly,
Let me be holding my lover or drinking my coffee.

Let us be drinking our coffee, unprepared.

Watch. Sooner or later the meeting will take place. We prepare by living our lives in the presence of God, knowing that the moment of dramatic incarnation of his presence may take place anytime. In the meantime, we live our lives knowing God is present in the ordinary, life-giving patterns of daily life: washing the dishes, patting the dog, holding our lover, drinking our coffee, unprepared.

This is how prayer happens. This is how God happens.

Behold, I bring good news of a great joy, which will come to all the people; for to you is born this day in the city of David, a Savior, who is Christ the Lord.

                        Luke 2:10, 11 (BCP, 75)

Christmas comes but once a year — and every day. Once upon a time at a certain hour of one day in the year of our Lord in a special place, God came into the life of his world. The moment that is Christmas remains a moment of overwhelming joy and hope and the promise of peace.

But that day and year and place and time are always. Phillips Brooks, the great preacher of the nineteenth century, put it this way:

Where children pure and happy pray to the blessed
    Child,
Where misery cries out to thee,
Son of the mother mild;
Where charity stands watching and faith holds wide
    the door.
The dark night breaks, the glory wakes, and
    Christmas comes once more.

IT HAD BEEN A LONG DAY, tedious, no surprises save unwanted and unwelcome challenges at work. He was tired of the whole thing. Finally, he had broken away and found his way home to a dark house. She was gone. There was no note. He had no idea where she might be.

He was standing at the kitchen sink, alone, washing out the last of the apple cider from a glass before he placed it in the dishwasher. He never heard her step as she entered the room, only the slight pressure of her arms reaching around to hold him. He turned, and they kissed. All was well.

This is how prayer happens. This is how God happens. The eighteenth-century poet Christopher Smart wrote,

> Where is this stupendous manger?
> Prophets, shepherds, kings, advise.
> Lead me to my Master's manger,

8

Show me where my Savior lies.
O the magnitude of meekness!
Worth from worth immortal sprung;
O the strength of infant weakness,
If eternal is so young!
God all bounteous, all creative,
Whom no ills from good dissuade,
Is incarnate, and a native
Of the very world he made.

*From the rising of the sun even unto the going down
of the same my Name shall be great among the Gen-
tiles, and in every place incense shall be offered unto
my Name, and a pure offering: for my Name shall be
great among the heathen, saith the Lord of Hosts.*

Malachi 1:11 (BCP, 38)

God the Creator becomes real in the world through the
incarnate presence of Jesus Christ.

THE JOB INTERVIEW was going well, until his interviewer asked,
"Tell me about your walk with Jesus."

The candidate replied without hesitation, "Every place I go,
Jesus seems to have arrived there first."

As he answered the question, he could see the interviewer's
eyes glaze over. What was expected was an affirmation of

personal piety. There was a long, painful silence, then the reply, "I'm not sure I understand. Tell me more?"

"Of course. You see, it's been clear to me since I first met Jesus that he's present in the world everywhere I go. You never know when and how he'll show up. It's God's world. Jesus Christ is God's presence in the world."

"Fine, fine," the interviewer broke in. "What I want to hear about is your walk with Jesus."

"That's what I'm talking about. My walk with Jesus doesn't depend on how good I am or how prayerful I am — only on God's presence in Jesus Christ. That has nothing to do with me. That's the work of God."

The subject was changed. The interview ended. The interviewer did not want to be told that Jesus is alive and well in the world. He wanted to hear the affirmation that when we are good enough and pious enough, *we* bring Jesus into the world — not the other way around. The story of Christmas and the reality of prayer are that God in Christ comes to us whoever we are, wherever we are.

> *If we say that we have no sin, we deceive ourselves,*
> *and the truth is not in us; but if we confess our sins,*
> *God is faithful and just to forgive us our sins, and to*
> *cleanse us from all unrighteousness.*
>
> 1 John 1:8, 9 (BCP, 38)

We wish it were not so. We wish that it only involved other people. It involves all of us.

Brother turns against brother, nation against nation. We turn away from those who are different from us and affirm only our own kind. Difference is dangerous. We loathe and avoid it, affirming what we know and those with whom we agree.

And when we do so, the ever-recurring and increasing cycle of evil is extended, until we fall on our knees and confess our own grievous fault. The truth is that sin dwells in us, and as it does, it is extended to others.

God is faithful and just to forgive us our sins and renew a right spirit within us. But first we have to ask for God's forgiveness — in prayer.

All we like sheep have gone astray; we have turned every one to his own way; and the Lord hath laid on him the iniquity of us all. Isaiah 53:6 (BCP, 39)

LOUISA IS TWO YEARS OLD. No child could be sweeter, more adorable, more loving — until the moment comes when she is thwarted and challenged.

Yesterday, her newest friend, Hannah, came to play. Hannah took one look at Louisa's new tricycle and moved across the room to climb aboard. "No!" screamed Louisa. "No! No! No! Mine! Mine!" There was much wailing and crying. Her mother rushed over to explain and to reassure Louisa. Once the little girl understood that her territory and property were not being taken from her, merely shared temporarily with her new friend, there was quiet and peace.

Louisa is not unique; she reflects clearly what each of us knows and wants: our own way, our own space, our own territory. Each of us turns again and again to claim what is ours. It is the human story — the story of the ages — that produces conflict, war and every kind of political problem.

The problem is evident in the day's news: the Israelis and the Palestinians, Republicans and Democrats, civil war in the Sudan, the Russians and the Ukrainians, the United States and global warming, the sense of rightness and entitlement evidenced by the French, the United Kingdom, the United States — virtually any and every nation.

We crave for a center, an absolute for our world and seek it in our own interests and in ourselves. There is but one absolute: God in Christ reconciling himself to the world. Jesus Christ was sent by God to change the way we understand and live in the world that God has made. This Jesus enters our world and intervenes on our behalf.

But this will only happen if you and I open our lives to Christ's presence in prayer — prayer made possible through Jesus Christ, our Lord.

The hour cometh, and now is, when the true worshipers shall worship the Father in spirit and in truth; for the Father seeketh such to worship him.

John 4:23 (BCP, 40)

"WHEN'S THE BEST TIME to trim that holly bush?" I asked my wise, older, and sometimes laconic, friend.

"When the shears are sharp."

12

When is the best time to pray, to practice the presence of God? There is no best time. All times are best; all times are right. God is always more ready to hear than we to pray.

HE AWOKE AS HE ALWAYS DID, very early, in the still dark small hours. Surrounded by unnamed and unknown fears, he remained very still hoping the fears would pass and prayed the familiar words, "Our Father, who art in heaven...." Then again, and again. Silence. He listened. God listened. It set the pattern for the day to be spent in the presence of God, always more ready to hear than we to pray.

This is how prayer happens. When prayer happens, the presence of God enters our lives, and God happens.

Thus saith the high and lofty One that inhabiteth eternity, whose name is Holy, "I dwell in the high and holy place, with him also that is of a contrite and humble spirit, to revive the spirit of the humble, and to revive the heart of the contrite ones."

Isaiah 57:15 (BCP, 40–41)

Strong, resounding words. Words that announce and demand silence. They are spoken and heard with the authority that comes from God and declares God's presence.

These words are associated from my boyhood with a small, well-known, imposing man, whose face was marked by a large aquiline nose that bespoke nobility. He called me by name, knew much about me, but remained distant, far removed from my world. These words, together with the passage from the book of Job when God speaks from the whirlwind, define this man. He proclaimed that God was real, God was imposing, God was distant, but God was always available and present, with us — in the silence.

Mother Teresa was asked what she said when she talked to God. "I don't say anything. I listen."

"Well, what does God say to you?"

Mother Teresa replied, "God doesn't say anything. God listens."

This is what happens in the silence when we practice the presence of God. God happens.

SHE PRAYED THE WORDS of St. Teresa of Avila:

May today there be peace within.

May you trust God that you are exactly where you are meant to be.

May you not forget the infinite possibilities born of faith.

May you use those gifts that you have received and pass on the love that has been given to you.

May you be content knowing you are a child of God.

Let this presence settle into your bones, and allow your soul
the freedom to sing, dance, praise and love.
It is there for each and every one of us.

Then she sat in silence, all alone, in the living room. Not a sound,
until she heard the dog whining in the back room, wanting to
go for her morning walk. Reluctantly, she rose, found the leash,
collected the tail-wagging golden retriever, and slipped out the
back door.

The morning light was barely evident, no car or person yet
abroad. She walked alone. Even the dog was quiet. All was quiet.
There was peace within and all around — everywhere. God was
present.

Chapter Two

ERRED AND STRAYED

Almighty and most merciful Father,
we have erred and strayed from thy ways like lost
sheep,
we have followed too much the devices and desires of our
own hearts,
we have offended against thy holy laws,
we have left undone those things which we ought to have
done,
and we have done those things which we ought not to have
done.
But thou, O Lord, have mercy upon us,
spare thou those who confess their faults,
restore thou those who are penitent,
according to thy promises declared unto mankind
in Christ Jesus our Lord;
and grant, O most merciful Father, for his sake,
that we may hereafter live a godly, righteous, and sober
life,
to the glory of thy holy Name. Amen.   (BCP, 41–42)

The Book of Common Prayer is introduced by the Opening Sentences. They begin the Daily Office, Morning and Evening Prayer, declaring that each day is lived in the presence of God. Once this is evident, our first act is to fall on our knees and confess that we have sinned.

That's not easy. It doesn't come naturally. How many times do you remember saying "I'm sorry"? Not many. We don't say so because we are not sorry. "Sorry? Sorry for what? Just what do you have in mind? I'm not sorry. Not me! You've got the wrong person! Find someone else, someone who's done something wrong."

The fact remains, however, that being sorry and saying "I'm sorry" are essential. All of us have sinned, fallen short, missed the mark. No association long continues until we acknowledge responsibility to be in relationship. A first step in our relationship with God is to acknowledge that *"we have erred and strayed from thy ways like lost sheep."*

In *The Story of the Bible* George Fabian Tittmann, a dynamic and commanding minister of the mid-twentieth century, taught me that if I had but a single hour to teach everything that is important about the Holy Bible, fifty-five minutes of that hour should be spent on the first three chapters of Genesis. Why? These three chapters establish the foundation for understanding the nature of the world and those who live in it. The first three chapters of Genesis assert:

- This is God's world.

- It is very good.

17

+ God has created and placed us in the world.

+ We want to place ourselves at the center of God's world.

+ God allows this.

+ There are consequences.

The metaphor that the General Confession uses to describe this is ancient, pastoral and rooted in the nomadic culture of our Hebrew ancestors. Their lives were defined by their work as shepherds. Sheep are not intelligent; they are single-minded, ornery and difficult to manage. Unless we live in rural, sheep-herding country, sheep are largely unknown to us, but their habits are uncomfortably close to our own. Most particularly and especially because *"we have followed too much the devices and desires of our own hearts."*

If there is one phrase that sums up the attitude of our time, it is: "It's all about me." We believe that the world begins, continues and ends with me, revolves around what I want, when I want it, and why I want it. This attitude fuels the world of advertising and our habits of consumption. We do what we want to do, go where we want to go, think what we want to think — when we want to, and because we want to do so.

Traditionally, this behavior and attitude is considered to have been created by "the Fall." The Fall occurred, according to the account in the third chapter of Genesis, when the serpent beguiled Eve into eating the fruit of the tree in the center of the Garden of Eden, the one thing that had been expressly forbidden by God. The serpent did so by tempting Eve, saying to her that if she ate, "You will be like God."

This fall away from the state of grace — that condition in which human beings had been created to live by God — had immediate, continuing and significant consequences. These are summarized in the word *separation*: separation from God, separation from one another and separation from one's self. The Genesis story describes the results of this separation: removal from the Garden, enmity among family members, conflict between human groups. The conflict between Jews and Arabs is but one consequence that the story Genesis tells. There are many others.

A cover of a paperback edition of Arthur Miller's contemporary play, *After the Fall* shows a cut-out figure of a human being that is falling. From the way the artist has drawn the cover, however, one cannot tell if the figure is falling down or falling up. Is it a Fall down, out of the state of grace, or is the Fall up into the state of existence that makes life possible?

Sin, the state of separation in which each individual and group lives, has dire consequences. It is also the source of human accomplishments, great and small. The drive to succeed, to explore, to invent, to solve problems, to grow nations and corporations all stem from the desire to be the center of our own world, to extend borders and test limits. The fact remains that the defining mark of the human condition is that *"we have offended against thy holy laws."*

The world in which we live is a world human beings have altered from the one given to us by God, the world created by God. Human beings, all of us, want things our way. One of Frank Sinatra's most memorable songs was "My Way." Sinatra did. So do we all. "It's all about me."

The ways in which we pursue a life that's "all about me" begin, continue and end in our willingness and God-given ability to offend against God's laws, the conditions set down for human existence that we continue to redefine to fulfill our own intentions.

"We have left undone those things which we ought to have done." This resonates with any thoughtful, reflective person. We know a great deal about those things we have left undone that we ought to have done. Each day is littered with their remains — the excuses we make to ourselves and others, each a variation of the ancient line, "I just couldn't stop myself."

WHEN HE ARRIVED AT WORK that Friday morning, there was the list he had created late the previous day, a neat catalogue of all the things he had vowed he would do on this day, the things left undone throughout the entire week. When he gathered himself together to leave the office on Friday afternoon, he had not completed a single item on the list.

AS SHE TURNED THE CORNER to walk down the main street of the small city, she saw the homeless man. Huddled off to the side, slouched in a doorway, eyes half open, three days' growth of beard, clothes dirty and disheveled, shoes untied — the bum was waiting, waiting to ask for a handout.

Walking faster now, faster and faster, looking down at her moving feet, she crossed the street and never looked back.

WHEN HE ARRIVED HOME later that same day, the sun had already set; the house was silent and dark. He picked up the day's mail that had fallen through the slot, went to his study, turned on a single light, opened each letter methodically, and began to read.

He heard her key turn in the lock, heard the door open, heard her footfall in the front hall. He spoke not a word and continued to read. It was ten minutes before she entered the study. He did not look up, nor did he speak.

And we have done those things which we ought not to have done. Those things we have left undone that we ought to have done are called sins of omission. Those we have done that we ought not to have done are called sins of commission.

Sin (spelled with a capital S) is a state of being. It is neither good nor bad. Sin just is. Sin is the way we are. On the other hand, *sins* (spelled with a small s) are acts, great and small, that we perform — whether through omission or commission. These sins result from Sin — our desire

21

to do what we want to do, when we want to do it. Sins separate us from one another, from our own true identity and from God. They come in various degrees of severity. Murder removes another human being from the face of the earth, but when we use a racial epithet, we do quite the same thing, for we make another human being less than human, and we turn that other person into a thing in our own estimation.

All have sinned and fallen short, as Jesus made clear in the Sermon on the Mount (Matthew 5:21–22), and all are in need of the grace and forgiveness of God. This is why we know that we need appeal to God in prayer by making a confession.

DRIVING TO WORK WAS STRESSFUL and such a waste of time. She wished she could avoid it, especially since it brought out the worst in her, made her angry, full of hate and discomfort.

This very thought crossed her mind, as she wove in and out of traffic on the freeway, annoying and cutting off as many people as possible. It saved time to be aggressive, rude, irresponsible, but it made her feel good, made her know she really was better than the others, the anonymous people, each making his or her own way down the highway, in their own small, private, enclosed world.

For a brief moment she wished this wasn't true, that she didn't need to think she was better than all the other people crowded in around her on this damned highway, each speeding along, alone.

She felt this only for an instant, but the fact that she felt it at all bothered her.

She arrived at the office late, as usual. Meg was standing behind her own desk, opening the morning's mail. She saw her out of the corner of her right eye, never broke stride, never spoke, didn't raise a hand or turn her head — just kept walking and closed the door of her office behind her.

Meg was a nuisance. Her husband was often away, on the road, visiting customers throughout the entire state as a manufacturer's representative. There were two teenage children, one in middle school and one in high school, that were driving Meg crazy. That was her problem. She'd dealt her own hand herself; now let her play it.

The phone was already ringing. She picked it up. Another day of work had begun. But the memory of non-encounter with Meg wouldn't go away, continued popping up in the forefront of her mind when she needed to concentrate on more important matters. It must have been ten o'clock when she finally got up from her desk for the first time, walked to the door, opened it and entered the outer office, as if to go get a cup of coffee or visit the restroom. Meg did not turn from her computer to face her. "Good morning," she said to Meg as she walked on by.

She wanted to do more. She knew that she should do more, but she just couldn't. She just couldn't.

The rest of the day was as dreary as the beginning had been. She felt awful. Wished she could go home. Wished she were dead. Wished...wished...she could speak to Meg. She couldn't and didn't.

(*And there is no health in us.*) This phrase was eliminated from The General Confession when The Book of Common Prayer was revised in 1979. It was removed because it was considered off-putting, offensive to normal, healthy people, especially younger people.

The use of the word *health*, however, has nothing to do with a medical condition. It is a translation of the word *salvus*, meaning "whole," the same root used in the word *salvation*. As a result of our own choice to be separated from God, from one another and even from our selves, we become far less than we might be. We are not whole. None of us is; although, surely, we each know persons who are on the one hand, less whole, and on the other hand, more whole, than all others. Some of us are truly pathetic, lost, miserable all of the time. "What a loser. He doesn't even know who he is." Others have succeeded in becoming more like the persons God made them to be. "She's a whole person," we sometimes say.

How does the latter happen? One has to believe that it is because some people are more honest, more willing to face their own shortcomings. When such people live with themselves as they truly are before God and self and neighbor, they are better able to minimize their shortcomings and become more of the persons they were created and intended to be. They are more whole. These are the people whom we most admire, the persons about whom we say, "I want to be like him when I grow up!" These are people of health, for they are whole.

These are the people whose ability to be honest with and about themselves involves the willingness and ability to confess that they have left undone those things they ought to have done, and done those things they ought not to have done.

But thou, O Lord, have mercy upon us. The power of the words, "I'm sorry" is beyond comprehension. The play *A Thousand Clowns* by Herb Gardner was the Pulitzer Prize winner in 1951. It continued for some time to appear on Broadway and was made into a successful film. The play concerns Murray, a free spirit and single parent who refuses to take a paying job to support his only son. Family Services, in the person of Sandy, a social worker, threatens to put his son in an institution, but still Murray is incapable of undertaking employment. The moment of truth comes. There must be a resolution, and in Murray's greatest speech of the play, quite like an aria in an opera, he says to Sandy, "I'm sorry. I'm sorry."

The play and its resolution turn on these two words. Once Murray asks for mercy and forgiveness, everything changes.

Our life of prayer, our moments and our days lived in the presence of God, hinge on our willingness and our ability to say, "I'm sorry." God will have mercy. Once we open the conversation, our life together really begins and continues.

Spare thou those who confess their faults. The fact is that once we say "I'm sorry" relationship then becomes possible. If we are penitent — and we want a new and healthier life — God is forgiving. Doors open. Life changes.

HE NEVER PLANNED THE AFFAIR. It just happened. Besides, he told himself, it didn't amount to that much. She was available, near at hand. There were glances, innocent conversations, a drink together, then dinner at a small neighborhood restaurant one night when his wife was out of town on business. After dinner, he walked her home and spent the night.

Once it had started, he didn't want to stop. Everything was easy, natural, expected; he just kept going with the flow. But the more he continued living the lie, the more it bothered him. He decided to speak to his best and oldest friend, his college roommate, and did so over lunch. Frank believed that it had to stop, and this would only happen if he confessed to Dolores. That was the last thing he wanted to do. It put his whole life at risk. But he did.

And she forgave him. She took him back, quoting their marriage vows, "for better, for worse." This was worse. It couldn't get any worse. Only now it got better, a lot better.

According to thy promises declared unto mankind. Such a situation is heart-rending, unbearable. But we've all been there. Not caught in an extramarital affair, but a responsible party to a broken relationship, an old friendship gone sour. Usually we do nothing, and then drift apart. Not so with God. God is there, always there.

In Christ Jesus our Lord. We know this thanks to the greatest story ever told, the story of our salvation, the birth of our freedom and wholeness in Christ Jesus, who was born and lived and suffered and died and was raised to new life for us. These events make possible the constant and continuing presence of God through prayer.

And grant, O most merciful Father, for his sake. For his sake, for the sake of Christ Jesus our Lord, we are "bold to say" (as the Prayer Book says) whatever our life of prayer demands, requires, and invites. Once we have entered the presence of God through confession, we are able to speak and listen freely, openly, gladly, in the full expectation *that we may hereafter live a godly, righteous, and sober life.*

Will we be perfect? Of course not. We shall again leave undone those things we ought to have done and do those things we ought not to have done. That is inevitable. But when this happens, we know the way back to the God who loves us and redeems us and gave Jesus Christ to be one with us.

Therefore, we know that everything we do, we do only *to the glory of thy holy Name.*

This is true because in the end — the very end — we do not live for ourselves. We do not live alone. We do not even die alone. We are bound to God, created by God, born to live finally with God, and to know the glory of his holy name.

What we know of this ultimate reality, this side of the grave, are only glimpses — vague, ephemeral, brief, vanishing. They are glimpses, not unlike the bare branches of trees in winter, as they first appear at dawn through the morning mist. The glimpse begins with a suggestion, a hint. If we are aware, our eyes and hearts open, then we shall see the presence of God.

The first time I met Bo Cox. I was scared. Everything was new and strange in the maximum-security prison, where Bo lived in Oklahoma, a state I had never visited. The unfamiliarity was very uncomfortable.

That was not all that was uncomfortable. Bo is intense, his eyes deeply set, his Oklahoma accent disarming. He is completely different from everything and everyone I have ever known.

But the real reason Bo makes me uncomfortable is that he speaks out of a long relationship with Jesus. Plain and unvarnished, what he says comes from deep within, from what he knows of Jesus and the life of prayer.

As Bo and I have talked, many times, I have said to myself. "Pay attention. Pay attention. It will never be any more real than it is right now. Jesus is part of this conversation, right here, with us."

That's not easy, not comfortable. Nor is prayer. Prayer is Jesus present, with us. Bo's conversation embodies the real and living presence of Christ Jesus. It's transforming, exciting and opens one to new opportunities. But it's never comfortable. The presence of Christ is life-changing.

Chapter Three

GUIDE OUR FEET

As Daily Morning and Evening Prayer near their close, there is a series of prayers known as Collects. A collect is a specified literary form containing an invocation, a petition and a pleading of Christ's name or an ascription to the glory of God. The name *collect* is assigned since it collects the petitions of several persons. The first collect in Morning and Evening Prayer is seasonal, to be discussed in the following chapter. The seasonal collect is followed by daily collects, offered to set the tone for this new day.

O God, the King eternal, whose light divides the day from the night and turns the shadow of death into the morning: Drive far from us all wrong desires, incline our hearts to keep your law, and guide our feet into the way of peace; that, having done your will with cheerfulness during the day, we may, when night comes, rejoice to give you thanks; through Jesus Christ our Lord. Amen.

(Collect for the Renewal of Life, 99)

The difference between night and day is a mystery. Some welcome it, but for me the dark offers a distorted way of seeing the world, misunderstanding the challenges ahead. As the Psalmist says, "Joy comes in the morning." Tears, distortion and the unknown mark the dark. From the dark we cry out to God, out of our aloneness, encased in misperceptions, believing that what is ahead is not good.

Morning brings the realization that God, who surrounds and uplifts us through all of time, will guide our feet into the way of peace.

AT FIRST LIGHT, we bundle up and walk for an hour on empty country roads — to listen. No street lights, no traffic, no sirens, no airplanes. We see and hear the silence before we become aware of the enormous sky, the hooting of great horned owls, the calls of geese, countless deer, and an occasional red fox far off in a barren field. Surrounded by the smell of woods, vivid colors, long grass whispers, far distant vapor trails high up and far off, we are most aware of the silence.

God is present. We watch, waiting, inside our own skins, knowing that God is the eternal, whose light divides the day from the night and turns the shadow of death into the morning.

Leo Tolstoy wrote in *Anna Karenina* that each day brings the possibility to follow our feet. We go where our feet take us; therefore, we begin this day asking God to guide our feet, guide them into the way of peace, guide them to those places where we may be whole and at one. Guide them with cheerfulness. Guide them so that we may gladly and freely greet the choice between joy and sadness that is within our power.

VERA POMEROY WAS THE YOUNGEST and only unmarried member of her large family. Crippled from birth, when the family decided they were no longer able to care for her, they consigned her to the County Home for the Crippled and Indigent. It was there I went to call on Vera.

The visits were a joy. It was as if I was actually doing something useful and important. Vera was a radiant person. Not that she was beautiful, hardly that, but she was radiant. Her face reflected a presence one seldom saw.

She was confined to her bed that was placed next to a window with a western exposure. Most afternoons, as I sat nearby, the sun was streaming onto her bed.

One afternoon, guilelessly and foolishly I said, "Vera, when I come to call, you are always so full of good cheer, smiling, upbeat. What is your secret?"

All she said was, "There is time enough to cry after you have left."

Those are words not to be forgotten. Spoken by a person whose life was lived by prayer, in the presence of God, who, in her paralysis, knew there were still choices that she could make for herself.

How we spend this new day is our choice. The tone is set as we awaken from the night to face the day. If we live the day with cheerfulness, when the night comes, we shall be able to rejoice, to give thanks to the God whose presence has guided our feet into the way of peace.

✠ O God, the author of peace and lover of concord, to know you is eternal life and to serve you is perfect freedom: Defend us, your humble servants, in all assaults of our enemies; that we, surely trusting in your defense, may not fear the power of any adversaries; through the might of Jesus Christ our Lord. Amen.

(A Collect for Peace, 99)

These words summon memories of occasions when I knelt in a congregation to settle into the real business of prayer. Over and over again in different times and different places, these words set the tone for God's presence.

O God, the author of peace and lover of concord. God, the creator of all that is, has many qualities, none more singular than these. This Collect declares that God is primarily the author of peace and lover of concord. "Author of peace" — not alone as the one who ends all conflict, although that too, but the creator of a world that is whole, at one, functioning as one world, the way it was created to be. It is a dream, as Martin Luther King Jr. proclaimed in his famous speech, and it is also a reality that we have glimpsed.

But to nail it home, to make the thought full and complete, we add, "lover of concord." The word *concord* means unanimity, agreement, consensus. It describes the world that God made, the world in which we were born to live. Early this day, we look forward to moments when we shall be at one not only with ourselves, but also with our best friend, our colleagues, and with the world where we live and work.

When I was responsible for the life and progress and good health of a community of five hundred people — teenagers and adults — brought together to learn as a school, it was my conviction that each day should begin with a community gathering. This was hardly an original idea, nor one with which many would disagree, but the demands of a daily schedule, a large enough physical space, and the general unwillingness of people to gather together in one place and one time did not make it easy.

We had to begin the day earlier than many wished; we had to build and pay for a special place; we had to fly in the face of prevailing opinion, for most other schools had given up daily assembly. I was insistent and single-minded that assembly would remain, and it did.

The school needed a powerful symbol that said, "As different and diverse as we are as a group, we shall gather together in one time and place, at the beginning of each day for a certain and sufficient period of time. Here we shall be together, with and for one another, to celebrate our wholeness, our oneness, our commonality. Once this has been done, then we shall go our separate ways and allow the day to unfold as it will, which is not necessarily as it should."

There were seldom, if ever, words of formal prayer in this gathering, yet all of it was a prayer for peace and concord. Since it was my creation and I was in charge, day after day, it made me very nervous, but the memorable moments, virtually daily, made it more than worthwhile.

- Stopping in mid-sentence, I looked up to see two seniors in conversation. Priding myself on the ability to call everyone by name, I called out, "Mr. Morse, just what are you and Mr. Little discussing so earnestly, while I am speaking?" "Actually, Mr. Gleason," he replied, "we are discussing how short your pants are." The place exploded with laughter, but a day had begun in peace and concord.

- Mary's mother died tragically and suddenly on Sunday afternoon. Such an unimaginable loss for an eleventh grade student had to be addressed. Halfway through my prepared remarks in that Monday morning assembly, I looked up to where Mary would normally have sat. To my great surprise, there she was, crying uncontrollably. Her presence made clear that in the midst of death there can be life — and peace and concord.

- Everyone loves to listen to a story read aloud. The memories and associations we all have with reading aloud are powerful; therefore, twice a month, I read aloud a favorite children's story. The same stories were repeated, year after year, as if they were liturgy, an expression of prayer.

THE EVENING WAS LOW-KEY — a quiet evening for four old friends who had not been together for more than a year. Grace was offered as they sat down around a wooden kitchen table, one candle in the center. The fare was simple: soup, salad, fruit, some cheese, a bottle of wine. The talk was of people they held in common, recent books and one film. Then there were stories of adventures shared in days gone by.

At the very end, they held hands and the host said, "We give thanks for this breaking of bread, for your presence in our midst, for the gifts of peace and friendship and lives shared through common hopes and common dreams. Amen."

Our lives are lived in the context of prayer.

To know you is eternal life. Eternal is beyond time. Neither past nor future, it happens in an unexpected moment and comes and goes before we realize it has happened. The eternal is an instant — the twinkling of an eye — defined by an event so daily and ordinary that it is otherworldly.

♦ Two-year-old Louisa was running for the front door, when she stumbled on the threshold, pitched forward and hit her head. A long silence, then the scream, as I pulled her from the floor and clutched her. We sat down together in the big red chair. Her sobs came ever more slowly. She dried her eyes. I kissed her.

- We stopped at the intersection as the squeal of the ambulance siren swished past us. It came and went almost before we noticed. Our prayers for the occupant, the EMTs, the doctors, and ourselves were silent.

- The morning sky was gray. Far, far away, small patches of blue and the glimmering light of the rising sun. The first group of twelve geese came from the south, the second, fewer in number, from the east, then from both directions at once. Fifty feet above the water, they wrapped their wings around them, stuck out their feet, plummeted down, down, down, first skidding then resting in the water, claiming it as theirs. The geese had come home for the morning.

When it surrounds us, the eternal becomes the only time there is. The future has not yet arrived; the past is gone forever. But both collide and combine to form the present. We pay attention, and we know — the eternal.

SOME MORNINGS, not every morning, just some, they lingered in bed, awake, together, talking, remembering, hoping, praying. The sheets were smooth and soft, the covers warm, the pillows soft. Each sentence, thought, memory, hope, was precious, singular, born of years of the closest kind of companionship. There was no other time, no opportunity quite like this, but this moment, this series of moments, defined their life together, those moments they had lived and those they would live — together and apart.

Prayer allows us to enter the eternal, the presence of God when we know in an instant that something unique is happening. It never happened before — not like this — it will never happen again. But right now, God is present. We are at prayer.

To serve you is perfect freedom. When Endicott Peabody founded Groton School in 1884 to transform the sons of the wealthy into men who would serve the greater good, he chose as the motto for his school a Latin translation of these very words from the Collect for Peace.

How many lives did Peabody change? No one knows. He profoundly influenced at least one: Franklin Delano Roosevelt. Whatever one's politics, it is clear that Roosevelt did much to transform the United States and to rescue the country, especially its most unfortunate citizens, from poverty and despair. He gave his life to serve. Crippled and disabled himself, he found a certain peace.

The idea that one may find perfect freedom by offering one's life up to the service of God is not easy to understand. "Freedom's just another word for nothing left to lose" were the memorable words of Kris Kristofferson's song of 1969, words made famous by Janis Joplin before her death. The song and the collect seem unrelated. Yet both say that the only way to live a life that is free and truly your own is to give it away. There will be no peace, no concord, no freedom until we allow ourselves to serve God. We find the will and the way to do this through prayer.

Defend us. The natural consequence of giving ourselves to God is that God defends us.

In all assaults of our enemies, the majority of which are self-created and self-inflicted, but God gives us the opportunity and responsibility to care for ourselves When John Kennedy began his term as president, he said, "Ask not what your country can do for you, but what you can do for your country." In most situations in which we find ourselves we are responsible for the outcome. We are the actors, not those who are acted upon. And we are not alone. God is present "to help those who help themselves" (Benjamin Franklin).

Surely trusting in your defense. Whatever hurts assail us, we are confident and secure in our life that is defined by the presence of God.

May not fear the power of any adversaries. Fear is the first and final enemy. Sometimes fear is real and well-founded. More often it is random and irrational. God's peace is freedom from fear — all fear. We are surrounded and upheld by the presence of God.

Lord God, almighty and everlasting Father, you have brought us in safety to this new day: Preserve us with your mighty power, that we may not fall into sin, nor be overcome by adversity; and in all we do, direct us to the

fulfilling of your purpose; through Jesus Christ our Lord. Amen. (A Collect for Grace, 100)

The very first moment after awaking every morning is a moment of grace. Grace is defined by the fact that none of us deserves anything. Life is a gift. We never asked to be born, but we were. Last night I fell asleep, perhaps easily, perhaps after tossing and turning, in the sure and certain hope that morning would come, and I would awake. This realization takes less than an instant, a microsecond, when I know that to be awake is a miracle, something I have come to expect. There is no reason to believe it will continue indefinitely.

Early yesterday morning, while I was still in the shower, the cardiologist called with the results of a nuclear stress test he'd administered to monitor the current state of my heart disease. "Things look good," he reported. "Much of it pretty normal, but then there is this one new small area of blockage. We'll have to watch that. If there are symptoms, we'll look again."

The last time — a decade ago — there were symptoms. My life was saved; death averted, for the time being. And so today in that microsecond of first awareness, I give thanks. Today is not *the* last day, but some day will be. Some day will be the day to say "good-bye."

Today, I have been brought in safety to this new day — a true, free gift — and so have you. What's to be done?

This Collect for Grace makes a series of suggestions: some obvious, others not at all.

✠ Now that we are awake and the day has begun, preserve us. Allow this day to continue. There are no guarantees. Each moment is a miracle. Remember me. May God, the power that gives life, uphold and preserve me and allow the rest of this day to happen.

There is no more basic attitude of prayer. You and I were conceived in grace. May it continue, not just this day but from this moment forward until the shadows lengthen and the evening comes and the busy world is hushed and our work is done and the day is over.

✠ May it continue not for any idle or passing fancy but with the hope that we may not fall into sin. May God who has restored me to life this day once again grant me the hope to live this day with him and without sin.

In the first blush of this new day, full of hope, awakening once again as if a child, I am brash enough and innocent enough to pray that God will grant me the special privilege of walking closer to the presence and power that makes life possible. Allow me to live this day with God and not only for myself. That would be a miracle. May it continue.

This is not a casual wish. Any moment, every moment, cherish what you have been given. This will only happen if we allow ourselves to practice the presence of God, to be immersed in prayer. It is no more difficult than the dictum of Alcoholics Anonymous: "let go and let God." It means emptying ourselves of what seems essential, so important to me, as I begin this day, and for one day, allowing this day to be lived with and for God. It is difficult and yet very easy.

 Suddenly aware of the swiftness and shortness of daily life, grant that this day, this one day — and then the next, and the next, and the next — may be devoted to God's purposes for my life.

WE ROUNDED THE BROAD TURN on the flat country road, failing to see that up ahead on the left, lying in the ditch, were the remains of a deer carcass. What remained of the dead body was completely covered by six immense turkey buzzards. The giant birds, who were as surprised as we were, rose in a mass from their morning meal, riding the air currents and attempting to avoid our rapidly approaching car.

The very last bird, barely and only at the very last moment, rode the current up and over our Honda. The wingspan was more than the width of the car. He looked to weigh at least a hundred pounds, as he came within inches of my face, separated from me only by the windshield. What if he had struck us?

It began and ended in an instant. One such instant will be the last.

 Heavenly Father, in you we live and move and have our being: We humbly pray you so to guide and govern us by your Holy Spirit, that in all the cares and occupations of our life we may not forget you, but may remember that we are ever walking in your sight: through Jesus Christ our Lord. Amen.   (A Collect for Guidance, 100)

Two phrases from The Book of Common Prayer are nearer to me than breathing. One is from The Burial of the Dead: "in sure and certain hope of the resurrection from the dead." The second is from this Collect for Guidance: "in you we live and move and have our being." These words define me. We are God's. Try as we may, important as it is to be our own person, we are God's.

SUNDAY AFTERNOON IN APRIL, alone in my dormitory study, there was a knock on the door. "Come in," I called and an advisee, a senior about to graduate, entered the room. Without introduction, he asked, "Do you know Tim Stokes who lives across the quad in Arundel?"

"No," I said, "But I remember seeing him playing bass in the group that jammed on the steps of the art gallery last Tuesday after dinner. Why do you ask?"

"His father just called to tell Tim that his fourteen-year-old brother had committed suicide. He's sitting over there in his room all alone. I thought you might want to go see him."

If I'd been honest, I could have said, "No, I really don't want to go see him; I have no idea what to say." But I went.

As I approached the door to the student's room, I wondered if I had the strength to lift my right hand and knock. A voice from far within the room said, "Come in." Tim was sitting at the opposite end of the room in an old mission-style wooden chair, nestled in the window alcove. As I walked into the room, he looked up and said, "Hi, Mr. Gleason." That was all. "Hi," I replied and sat down on the bed.

"Tough news. Do you have any details?"

"Shot himself." There was silence. Mostly I remember only the silence. We both continued to sit there, averting our eyes. Occasionally, I caught a glimpse of him looking at the floor. After a while, he turned and looked out the window.

"Look," I said. "I'd like to say something that would make everything all right. But I can't. There are no such words. So what I did come to say is this. I'm sorry. Sorry more than I can say. Everyone you know in this school—and they are many—is sorry. They all know, all of them. And they don't know what to say. So let me say this for them. Take care, for we care for you and for your brother. Wherever he is, he's in God's hands. And so are you."

As I stood and turned to leave, I said, "If you want to talk more, you know where to find me." I opened the door and fled.

Tim and I never saw one another again, not to this day, but last year he wrote me a letter out of the blue. The letter said, "Thank you. You'll never know how much your visit meant."

In you we live and move and have our being. God is always present. Even when prayer is wordless, God's presence makes it possible. Knowing this, we are confident God will *guide and govern us . . . that in all the cares and occupations of our life . . . we may remember that we are ever walking in your sight.*

43

"Coincidence is God's way of remaining anonymous." The statement is a compelling summary of the conclusion of this collect. No one of us has ever seen God or engaged in conversation with God, yet time and time again we are assured of God's presence through the unexplainable chain of events that change lives; therefore, coincidence is God's way of remaining anonymous.

Despite our attempts to find a scientific explanation for the attraction between men and women, one of the abiding mysteries of human life is what makes two people fall in love. What makes two people really, truly, fall in love — not just an affair, a mere fling highlighted by sexual attraction — but love that lasts and lasts through years and years of committed, faithful marriage?

This is one of the ways in which God intervenes in our lives, remaining anonymous, and we are left with the sure and certain conviction that God does guide and govern us in all the cares and occupations of our life. We are truly walking in God's sight. And so we continue to pray.

Lord Jesus Christ, you stretched out your arms of love on the hard wood of the cross that everyone might come within the reach of your saving embrace: So clothe us in your Spirit that we, reaching forth our hands in love, may bring those who do not know you to the knowledge and love of you; for the honor of your Name. Amen. (A Collect for Mission, 101)

Jesus, the Son of the Living God, the anointed one, the Christ, died for every one of us. Not just you or I, who know him as the Lord of all life, but every person who crosses our path this day, every day.

His arms stretched out on the cross, open wide for all persons to come to him. But, as we see Jesus bound to his cross, he is immobile. He has no arms but ours to embrace the world and bring its people into his presence. This we are asked to do. This we seek to undertake. It is not easy or natural to offer ourselves and the saving love of God in Christ to others. We may be afraid, lack confidence or consider ourselves above it all.

THE WAITING AREA WAS CROWDED, without any seats available. They sat on suitcases. Hungry, tired, irritated, annoyed, he wanted to get on with the day. She was silent.

He amused himself by looking around, speaking to himself, and then out loud, making derogatory remarks about first one person and then another. She pretended not to hear, but he became more and more outrageous, until she could contain herself no longer.

His final comment had been directed toward a person with a disability. The description included a reference to a "chimpanzee." She turned, faced him, smiled, and said, "Christ died for that person."

Lord Jesus Christ, you stretched out your arms of love on the hard wood of the cross that everyone might come within the reach of your saving embrace. His arms enclose us all, those we love, those we hate, those we believe are less than we are. How do we become aware of this? By looking around and realizing that Christ died for each and every one of us. His arms stretch out to the world near at hand and the world far away at every moment. All are equal in his love, all gain worth through his love. All deserve to know of that love. They will not know unless we tell them. Give us the strength, we pray, to tell them, offer to them the arms of love that have embraced us.

So clothe us in your Spirit that we, reaching forth our hands in love, may bring those who do not know you to the knowledge and love of you. All we need do is to open our arms in love just as he opened his in death. This is one reason that the cross is the symbol of our life of faith and prayer. In its strength we open ourselves, stretch wide our arms in love to those whom we meet, those we know and those who are complete strangers.

For the honor of your Name. Amen. Every prayer ends in the name, power and strength that are ours in the new life we receive through Christ the Lord. His presence makes everything possible: prayer and its results in each moment of our daily lives.

Chapter Four

THE TIME OF THIS MORTAL LIFE

During each season of the Christian year, a collect that defines the essence of the season is assigned to be prayed during the Daily Office or the Holy Eucharist.

Almighty God, give us grace to cast away the works of darkness, and put on the armor of light, now in the time of this mortal life in which your Son Jesus Christ came to visit us in great humility; that in the last day, when he shall come again in his glorious majesty to judge both the living and the dead, we may rise to the life immortal; through him who lives and reigns with you and the Holy Spirit, one God, now and for ever. Amen.

(First Sunday of Advent, 211)

Advent is a new year, a new time. Advent is the *now* of our life, this mortal life, transformed into a new dimension, transformed into holy time. Holy time has a beginning in God's creation and an ending. It has been intersected and changed by the advent of Jesus Christ. Christ enters our daily life. Daily life is circular, repetitious, goes on and on, one thing after another, after another, after another, year after year.

But *now* it is Advent, a new dimension. In the fullness of holy time everything we know is transformed by a one-time event that makes all this difference: the birth of Jesus Christ.

Daily time is circular: a single center around which everything revolves, over and over and over again. Holy time is quite different from the circle; it is a straight line with a beginning and an end. It is transformed by Christ's advent into a new dimension. Advent announces this change that begins at Christmas, when Christ appears and is further marked by Christ's Resurrection at Easter. Christmas and Easter provide two foci for a new understanding of holy time.

Advent announces that Jesus is coming. He comes not through any action of our own. Advent happens, and when Jesus comes at Christmas, our mortal life is dramatically changed forever. Jesus Christ, the Son of God, comes to visit us in great humility. He comes once, for all time, as a human being who will share our life in every detail.

The cornerstone of the Christian faith is the Incarnation: God made flesh, God and man in one person. The incarnation is a paradox: two contradictory truths held to be present and true at one time and in one person. It has never happened before. It will never happen again. This paradox is not easy to understand, unique, in the proper and seldomly used sense of that word. It happens once and for all time.

What in the world — your world — could that have to do with your life of prayer? How could that translate into the practice of finding the presence of God?

SHE WAITED, ALL ALONE, in the silence, listening for any indication — a single small suggestion — of what made her life special, different, holy, set apart. The phone rang, the last thing she wanted or expected. As she rose and walked across the room, she looked at her watch. Ten-thirty. Pretty late for any one to call. She picked up the receiver in mid-ring. The voice said, "Hi, Mom. I hope I didn't call too late. I just got off the plane here in Denver. I'm here for a week, all alone. We've got a new start-up, and they sent me to supervise getting it up and running.

"But that's not why I called. Oh, before I start, how are you anyway? I should have asked that first."

"Fair to middling. My headaches have started again. Nothing helps."

"I'm sorry. Really sorry. Wish I had a magic pill I could send with an e-mail. But let me tell you why I called. On the way out on the plane I sat next to a guy; he was a complete stranger. We started to talk. Or, I should say, he started to talk. I wanted to read, and besides I never want to talk on airplanes. But he wouldn't stop."

"So what did you talk about?"

"That's why I called. He got me talking — about myself. Question, after question, after question. I wanted to ask him to shut up, but the questions were too interesting. Said he was writing a book on what makes each person different, really different, one from the other.

"So he asked where I was born, grew up, went to school — all the standard stuff. He kept pushing and pushing and pushing. Said he really needed answers for his book. 'Sam,' he said, 'what makes you different?' Finally I had to tell him.

"I said, 'Let me tell you about my mother. She's like no other person in the world. Why? I suppose it's because she really understands me. Knows me, through and through, and loves me still and all. No one else, at least no one else I ever knew, has a mother like that.

"'And that made a difference, a huge difference while I was growing up. Come to think of it, it makes a huge difference right now.'

"Meanwhile, as I kept talking and talking and talking, he didn't say anything. Not a word. We flew on in silence. I went back to my book, until five minutes later, right out of the blue, he said 'Thank you.' That was all, just 'Thank you.' The conversation was over.

"So when I got off the plane, something told me to call you up."

All her mother could say was, "Thank you, Sam. Thank you."

The difficulty we experience with the reality of incarnation is not only that God himself would come to visit us, but that God would visit us as a human being. When we fail to understand the incarnation, our chief difficulty is realizing that Jesus is fully human. Jesus did not just *seem* to be human. Jesus was human, like you and me, and came to visit us in great humility. The key word is *humility,* which means, "of the earth" — no pretense, fully human, not phony, the real thing.

> *Let the same mind be in you that was in Christ Jesus, who, though he was in the form of God, did not regard equality with God as something to be exploited, but emptied himself, taking the form of a slave, being born in human likeness. And being found in human form, he humbled himself and became obedient to the point of death — even death on a cross.*
>
> Philippians 2:5–8

The example we are offered in the person of Jesus is beyond our grasp and is more than we can fully comprehend, but it is an example of how human life should be lived. What this means, among many other things, is that every time we pray, we pray in the name of Jesus Christ, through Jesus Christ, because of Jesus Christ, who shared this life — our life — with us and for us as a human being.

This is not all. The Collect for Advent goes on to say: *in the last day, when he shall come again in his glorious majesty.* The two highlights of the Christian year that begins in Advent are Christmas and Easter — two complimentary but different events. Time has been transformed and is no longer circular and repetitious. It has a beginning, announced in Advent and realized in Christmas. It also has a goal: the resurrection at Easter. There is inexorable progress from life, through death, into the new life of Easter. Our life in Jesus Christ has meaning. Life has purpose and direction that begins as we await and then experience the birth of Christ and concludes in the new life Christ has made possible for us beyond the grave when *we may rise to the life immortal.*

The new life that awaits us — the life of the resurrection — is the most difficult to understand of all the realities in the Christian faith. Nor shall we finally understand it until we fully experience it ourselves.

Nonetheless, there are small events that provide a taste of what is to come. Each and every one of them is marked by anticipation — waiting — which is the central experience of Advent. We spend four weeks waiting, exploring the rich and multifaceted aspects of this mortal life that will ultimately usher us, fully born anew, into the new time that awaits us in the life of the resurrection.

Upstairs in what was once the attic of the house where I grew up was a spare room, sparsely furnished with a painted brass bed, bureau, desk, two chairs and a rope rug. It was my mother's spare room, far removed from the rest of the house, where she would undertake an occasional sewing project.

One day I discovered, quite by accident, that this was the room where mother gathered the Christmas presents. She arrayed them in neat piles arranged by recipient. Christmas was a family affair, but mother was Santa Claus.

As the much younger child, I was often left alone — all alone — in the house. Temptation was overwhelming. I would tiptoe, up, up, up the stairs and then down the long corridor to the closed door of the spare room, open it, slowly, silently, to feast my eyes, then my hands. I did this frequently through three different pre-Christmas seasons.

Somehow my mother figured this out. On the Christmas morning when I was twelve years old, when I descended the stairs at four o'clock in the morning to examine what Santa had spread around the Christmas tree, there was not a single present for me.

Surely there was some mistake. After the rest of the family arrived, more presents would surely materialize. Only they did not. I tried to remain calm, retreated behind a shell, sitting alone in the corner of the room. Mother pretended not to notice.

My discomfort was so intense, so excruciating, it has blocked all memory of the pain. What I do remember is that at long last my mother made a short, loud speech about the absence of my presents. She asked me to accompany her to an adjacent hall closet. I would rather have run away. When she opened the door, there was the pile from the spare room, still unwrapped, all recognizable, since I had seen and touched every one. She bade me help her place my presents under the tree. I did so. That was all there was to it. Amidst the cries of "Oh" and "Ah" and "Can you believe it?" nothing else was said or done. The genius of the punishment was that it was never explained. What it was intended to mean was left for me to conclude. What I concluded through my anguish is that if life is to be fully lived, it is to be marked by anticipation. It is anticipation that fully colors each present moment.

The essential color and beauty that is given to each of us in every moment of every day and every year is hope. This hope is gratifying. This hope is reliable, but if it is to be hope in its fullness, then it remains unknown. We can anticipate it, be enlivened by it, but we shall not know it in its fullness. It remains only to be fully known in the new life that we shall finally enter when we know and experience the resurrection of our Lord Jesus Christ, whose Advent is described in this collect.

Almighty God, you have given your only-begotten Son to take our nature upon him, and to be born of a pure virgin: Grant that we, who have been born again and made your children by adoption and grace, may daily be renewed by your Holy Spirit; through our Jesus Christ, to whom with you and the same Spirit be honor and glory, now and for ever. Amen. (Collect for Christmas Day, 213)

Christmas is what makes it possible for us to pray. Christmas is a paradox. God enters our lives at Christmas as one of us. He takes our nature upon him to live his life for us. But this is only half of the story. The other half is that Jesus is born of a pure virgin. Jesus is born a human being, but he is like no other. His birth is a miracle, a paradox. It never happened before or since. He is a human being conceived by God, his mother a pure virgin, who has "known not" a human father.

My late mother-in-law, who was a woman of clear, even luminous, faith, stood in the pew, Sunday after Sunday, unable to recite the creed. The virgin birth made no sense to her. Of course it made no sense. It is not intended to make sense. The virgin birth is the Christmas story told and retold that all may see and believe. Jesus was man who took our nature upon him, but he was also God, born of a pure virgin.

There is no way to illustrate the Christmas story. It is not "like" any thing else. It is unique. And it is the uniqueness of Christmas that makes it possible to pray. Christmas opens the way for our prayer. How is that so? Jesus Christ lived our human life with us and for us. Jesus knows us as we know ourselves. Jesus, who is the Son of God, welcomes us nearer into the presence of God. That presence is the life of prayer.

HIS FATHER HAD BEEN DEAD for fifty years but his presence remained as real as in the days when their conversations were daily. There was always a distance between them; this father and son were not intended to be best friends. There are some who say, "Why, my dad was my best buddy!" Not so for these two. The distance between them, however, was pervaded by warmth. Their love was palpable, often sealed with a kiss.

His father's love provided a special freedom, freely and openly granted. It was frequently true that his father's wisdom, insight, and open communication were readily available, never covered by silence. Still, no choice was predetermined, and each choice belonged to the son.

His father's words, "You know what I think. You know what I would do, if I were you, but it's your life. You decide. I'll support your decision," were spoken frequently.

None was more significant than when the son came home to announce what he had decided to do with his life. He called ahead, chose the time carefully, and entered the house without making a sound. His father was home alone, seated in the sunroom, reading *The Wall Street Journal.*

When not yet thirty years old, the father had started a small real estate business that grew into an empire. No wish was dearer to the father's heart than the hope that his son would join him and eventually take over the business.

It was not a comfortable time. Distance was more evident than warmth, but neither man was uncomfortable.

"Dad," the son began, "I've made up my mind. It hasn't been easy, but I've decided to apply to graduate school and study philosophy."

"What in the world for?"

"To teach. I want to teach and write, be a scholar."

"You won't make a dime."

"No doubt. I've thought about that. I know this is a great disappointment to you, and I'm sorry."

"Well, don't be. It's your life. You'll still inherit the business some day. Sell it. Or get someone else to manage it. Either way, it'll support you, make it possible for you to do what you want. It's meant a lot to me, but what the hell. There's more to life than real estate."

The son had just entered graduate school when his father died, prematurely and unexpectedly. Every single day that conversation is prominent in his mind, motivating and making possible everything the son undertakes. His father's continued presence and permission remained real, allowing the communication that empowered ongoing life.

Christmas reminds us that God is with us in the person of Jesus Christ and we have been born again. The realization is vital. We have been born again not because of anything that any of us has done, but thanks to Jesus Christ into whose life, death and resurrection we have been born through baptism, through the gift of grace first received at Christmas.

We, who have been born again once and for all time, experience this reality again and again, in small ways and large, through new beginnings, new opportunities, new expressions of our daily life.

Therefore, since we have been made God's children by adoption and grace through baptism and the gift given to us at Christmas, we pray that we may daily be renewed by the Holy Spirit. As we pray, daily renewal happens.

Sometimes this experience turns our life upside down; the change is massive.

Nothing about his death was easy, but one thing was very clear. George's death was a victory. He was eager to be with Jesus, for he has been with Jesus for many years already.

He was a man whose life was marked by new beginnings. Every day brought one. Every occasion when you met or talked with him brought one. Some were bigger than others: his conversion to Christ, his sobriety, his marriage, his children, the foundation he established to help individuals and groups confront alcoholism.

He first received Jesus Christ drunk and in a jail cell. At three o'clock in the morning, his rector arrived and said to him, "The only reason I'm here is because Jesus Christ loves you." His new life in Christ began right then, and it never ended.

Being born again is always transforming but there are times when it happens simply — in the quiet, daily unfolding of our lives. The result is the same: we are changed.

A dear friend wrote,

FIVE YEARS AGO I had an operation on my spinal chord. When my rector heard about it (I didn't tell him), he visited me before the operation. We discussed my surgery and whether I wished to be on the list of intercessions. My wife and I had made a decision not to tell too many persons about the operation. We prayed; we knew we had the rector's prayers, and somewhat reluctantly agreed to be on the parish intercession list. But I didn't talk too much about the operation. I was certain that I could handle it by myself with my wife's help.

It was a major operation that lasted fourteen hours, and I was hurting when it was over. Three days later my recovery slowed, and, suddenly, I believed there was no hope and wanted to die. My prayers had not worked, and I had been deserted by God. My world had gone totally dark and despair was my only thought. I had prayed hard, my family had prayed hard, and I thought that I was ready for this, but my world had gone totally dark.

Then I asked to see a hospital chaplain, and shortly one appeared—a Jesuit priest. He looked at me and said, "My son, we have taken over for you. We are praying for you. Let us do it." Then he held my hand for a long time, prayed, and left. Suddenly, the room had color. I was relaxed. I stopped worrying. Everything would be all right. I knew that I would live. My life had gone from darkness to light.

Fifteen minutes after the chaplain had left, my parish priest was at the bedside. My wife arrived a few minutes later, and we had communion together. I told my story, cried, and we all prayed together. The words of the Jesuit have stuck with me. "We have taken over. We are praying for you. Let us do it."

O God, by the leading of a star you manifested your only Son to the peoples of the earth: Lead us, who know you now by faith, to your presence, where we may

see your glory face to face; through Jesus Christ our Lord, who lives and reigns with you and the Holy Spirit, one God, now and for ever. Amen. (Collect for the Epiphany, 214)

Manifest, whether used either as a verb or a noun, is not a word we hear frequently. *You manifested your only Son. Manifest* is a word inextricably related to the Feast of the Epiphany. This is the season when Jesus is manifested, which means, "made evident, unmistakable, visible" to the world.

During my tour as a naval officer I served on ships that carried cargo and troops on specific missions. The operations officer (the person in direct charge of all details of the ship's assignment) would be equipped with a manifest. The manifest was a document that listed in complete detail every person and every article taken aboard for a specific mission. The operations officer stood at the gangway wherever material was being loaded to check everyone and everything taken on board.

Epiphany is the season when Jesus Christ is made manifest. In Epiphany it becomes clear what will take place in the mission and ministry of Jesus Christ. This is announced *by the leading of a star.*

The leading of a star is not an everyday event. Epiphany is unusual, set apart, the time when Jesus and those who follow him reach out to change the world. It happens by the leading of a star. There is a vision, an idea; at first there is a suggestion and then a glimmer that leads to new horizons.

The life that has never been led by a star — a vision that compels us to follow — is no life at all. The vision of the star enters our life through prayer, or one may say that when the vision appears, that is prayer. Do we have the eyes to see, the ears to hear and the heart to understand?

THE GREEN WALL PHONE on the far side of the kitchen had just started to ring as she pushed open the door and struggled into the room, balancing three packages and her briefcase. She dropped them all right next to the kitchen island and picked up the phone on the fourth ring.

"Mum," the voice said, "I need to come home for a talk — just the two of us. It won't take long. [Pause.] Well, it might take a while, come to think of it. Do you have any time after supper? Just for the two of us?"

She did have plans for the evening but knew in an instant that none was as important as responding to this call. "Sure, sure," she said. "What time?"

"I could get there by eight. I'll bring some Pepsi and a thermos of coffee."

When the daughter walked through the door a little before eight, her mother was sitting off in the alcove at the round blue kitchen table, working on her reports. She stood; they greeted one another with a kiss and an embrace that were easy and natural.

"So what's up?"

"I want to know if I'm in love. How do I tell?"

They both sat down at the same time.

"How did you know? How did you first know that you were in love with Dad? What made it different?"

"There had never been anyone else. No one. He was it. And I knew. I just knew. So did he."

"So how am I supposed to know?"

"You just will. How are you feeling right now?"

"I think this is it. I really do. But I want to be sure, really sure."

"I'd like to say something poetic and profound and wise and wonderful — just to be alliterative — but even if I could and did that wouldn't help. No one else can help. You'll have to decide. But I'll say one thing more. You wouldn't have come all this way to sit down with me if you weren't sure already."

Minutes later, as the daughter pushed open the storm door and headed for her car, she turned and called over her shoulder, "Love you, Mum."

The following words were written to me by my wife, shortly after we had become engaged and one year prior to our marriage.

There was a blinding
Light from the stone
You have given me.

It first came as white light
And then as I watched it
It changed color
Clear and brilliant

A red
A pure green
A blue
A yellow

And then it went away
But in that moment
I knew our Love
Was as pure
And radiant as that gleam
And that I need never be afraid
For God had shown
His love in that light
And together we would strive for the Light and Truth
And when the way grows dark
We will take a minute
And remember
And once again
        See the Light.

Epiphany is not a private event. The manifestation is to the world, *to the peoples of the earth*. When the most spectacular, life-changing event imaginable has taken place, it is not a private matter but needs to be shouted from the rooftops.

Politics may be too mundane, too worldly, to be considered in this context, but the 2004 presidential election is a case in point. In Ohio, where many believe the election was actually won and lost, several well-informed, hard-working Democrats, when asked what really happened, said, "The Republicans ran a better race. They were better organized, more passionate, worked harder. They believed more in what they were doing and why, and they reached out to more prospective voters and convinced them of the rightness of the Republican cause."

Epiphany is not a private event. It has to be proclaimed. "If you build it, they will come," is only partly true. People have to be invited if they are to come. Another person must reach out to them to tell, inform, and invite.

What is frightening about the contemporary understanding of marketing is that whatever the product is that is being marketed, its creator will gladly alter and package the product to serve the desires and needs of the customer. This is not the case when the product is Jesus Christ. Alteration is not necessary, but announcement is mandatory.

That announcement *to the peoples of the earth* is the joy and responsibility of those to whom the gift has been given, those to whom the Lord Jesus has been sent, those who have heard and seen and understood. It is we who spread the word thanks to the fact, as this collect states, that God has seen fit to *lead us . . . to your presence.*

This is the definition of prayer. Prayer happens whenever God leads us and we follow into the presence. If we are to know and be known by God in Christ and proclaim what we know to others, then prayer happens when we allow ourselves to live in the presence. The opportunity is always available, but the choice is always ours. God is ever-present, but we have to open ourselves to God's presence. Whenever we do, we are at prayer.

✠ **Almighty and everlasting God, you hate nothing you have made and forgive the sins of all who are penitent: Create and make in us new and contrite hearts, that we, worthily lamenting our sins and acknowledging our wretchedness, may obtain of you, the God of all mercy, perfect remission and forgiveness; through Jesus Christ our Lord, who lives and reigns with you and the Holy Spirit, one God, for ever and ever. Amen.**

(Collect for Ash Wednesday, 264)

The Collect for Ash Wednesday assumes that we shall look deeply and honestly within ourselves, knowing that God will *hate nothing [he has] made.*

God is different from us and stands apart from us; therefore, Lent will lead to new life and renewal (which is a definition of the word *Lent*) of all that we undertake. Life brings promise, if first there is honesty.

The world is full of children who have been abused, most often by their parents, those who created them. The world is full of despair, people depressed by the mess they have made of their own lives through shortsightedness, addiction, or dishonesty. But the Ash Wednesday Collect begins with the affirmation that the God who made us hates nothing in the world God has made — not even you and me.

Everyone faces the end of life, the moment when we must release all control. A friend of many years wrote a letter in which he reflected on this clear and certain fact.

Just before Christmas, as I was being shuffled in and out of operating rooms, MRIs and CT scans, and things were looking grim, I had time to think and pray about the unknown, the indecision that faced us. Suddenly there were two words I focused on: *path* and *journey*. If I truly believed in God, then I must follow the *path* — the Way that God had given me to follow. I need not fear it. God has watched over me and has already made that decision. The *journey* has been rich and wonderful, and if it is to stop now . . . so be it. I suddenly stopped worrying, stopped worrying completely. I never gave the cancer concerns another thought. I just knew that I was on the *journey* that had been set aside for me — come what may.

Knowing that God hates no part or person in the whole creation places our life in God's presence on a whole new level. Nothing shall separate us from God, for God *forgive[s] the sins of all who are penitent*. Nothing can separate us from God when we are sorry.

"I'm sorry." Not easy words to say, but they are the words that heal all relationships, including our relationship with the God who made us and loves us.

Consider the pivotal words of the Ash Wednesday Collect: *create and make in us new and contrite hearts*. Life is full of promise and a new beginning if we are contrite: apologetic, humbled, remorseful, repentant, regretful, sorry. We cannot do it alone, and so we ask God, in prayer, to create in us new and contrite hearts, *lamenting our sins and acknowledging our wretchedness.*

Once we are clear, honest, and straightforward, we may *obtain... perfect remission and forgiveness.* Perfect means complete, absolute, full. Or, to put it another way, we have become whole and new. This the promise of Lent, the season we enter through the gateway provided by Ash Wednesday, a day that is every day in our life of prayer.

> May today there be peace within.
> May you trust God that you are exactly where you
>   are meant to be.
> May you not forget the infinite possibilities that are
>   born of faith.
> May you use those gifts that you have received,
> And pass on the love that has been given to you.
> May you be content knowing you are a child of
>   God.
> Let this presence settle into your bones,
> And allow your soul the freedom to sing, dance,
>   praise and love
> It is there for each and every one of us.

IT WAS JUST AN ORDINARY DAY, a day like every other day. Driving up the interstate between courtesy calls on customers—more of the same old, same old. Then for no reason he could imagine or remember, it came like a flash, a vision from no where and for no reason.

Reminiscent of a rhyme from childhood, the words went something like this: "I may not be all I ought to be, and I'm sure not all God meant me to be. But I am who I am. This is the only day I have—today. And you know what? That's good. In fact it's better than good. Thank you."

 O God, who for our redemption gave your only-begotten Son to the death of the cross, and by his glorious resurrection delivered us from the power of our enemy: Grant us so to die daily to sin, that we may evermore live with him in the joy of his resurrection; through Jesus Christ your Son our Lord, who lives and reigns with you and the Holy Spirit, one God, now and for ever. Amen.

(Collect for Easter Day, 222)

Grant us to die daily . . . that we may evermore live with him in the joy of his resurrection. No words come closer to describing the essence of the Christian faith. Everything about our life as Christians points to and radiates from Easter. It begins with death, but death is never the end.

BORN IN 1861 on a farm near Monkton, New Brunswick, Canada, one of nine children, my grandfather, Bapapa (whose real name was Job), attended a local business college, then moved to Boston, met and married my grandmother, who was from Maine. He was bright and handsome, personable, engaging. He started a small real estate and insurance business and was unusually successful for a young man who began with nothing. He prospered, moved to better and better neighborhoods, sent his daughter to Girls' Latin, the best girls' school in the country, and then to Smith College. When she married, he built her a new house nearby. Bapapa knew a thing or two about control.

Then came the Depression. Bapapa was in his late fifties, and he lost everything. His business was gone. He was wiped out. He started all over, created a new business, purchased new and different, small, unusual properties, one at a time. Each property was located in or near Park Square, which he maintained was the direction of the future. It was where the new city of Boston finally did move, but not until some forty years after his death, and by then his descendents had sold all the property. When Job Gaskin died, the man I called Bapapa, one would not have called him wealthy, but he did leave a modest estate and a great deal for me to think about when I stop to look at the photographs of him that line our walls.

At the time of his death, my grandfather had worked more than thirty-five years *after* becoming bankrupt and losing everything. He never retired, never wanted to retire. He went to a favorite vacation hotel in Florida in the winter months where, day after day, he played bridge with countless lady friends and to another such hotel in Maine for a few weeks each summer. Otherwise, he was in his office at 224 Stuart Street virtually every working day. I never dared ask him if he believed the pattern and outcome of his life had been shaped by his bankruptcy at mid-life and the absolute necessity to start all over again at a time when most persons are getting ready to stop work. Motivation was never an option or a question. Or was it? Some driving force entered his life and changed it. It was the power of Easter. Out of death — bankruptcy — came new life. He could have just given up. He didn't. He was raised up.

"New every morning is the love our wakening and uprising prove." The first line of John Keble's memorable hymn speaks of every morning. Mornings are marked by Easter. Easter is the ever-present reality of our lives. Everything that begins, ends. Death happens. Nothing — no person, no job, no friendship, no institution — is forever. We all know this; nonetheless, we live most of our lives in denial, which is folly.

But there is more, much more. This conviction continues and concludes. Every ending contains the promise of a new beginning.

Life is driven by renewal, the persistent energy of rebirth that makes all things new. Pain and loss and death are inevitable, but each and every time they happen, there will be new life. Death happens, but it is never the final answer.

Everything that begins ends, and every ending contains the promise of a new beginning. This conviction makes human life possible. It is the ultimate cornerstone of our life of prayer: the presence of God.

ON A TUESDAY MORNING in February during a six-month sabbatical we spent in Santa Fe, I was writing a book. It was going well, but on this particular morning at about ten o'clock I needed to get away and reflect. I took a morning walk downtown.

As I walked home, a pickup truck, bearing the inscription PIDGEON DELIVERY SERVICE, INC., came down the hill and suddenly swerved across the street to pull in against the curb next to me. The driver opened the door on my side and said, "Excuse me for minding somebody else's business, but you look like a fella having an argument with himself."

"As a matter of fact," I replied, "I'm trying to figure out what to do with the rest of my life."

Richard reached across the seat. We shook hands and said, "Good morning." Although we did not know one another, we had met more than once at the seven o'clock Wednesday morning service at The Church of the Holy Faith. Dick and four generations of his family had lived all their lives in New Mexico. I felt comfortable with Dick. It felt like he owned this place, so new to us, so familiar to him.

"Well," he continued, "What are the possibilities?" I told him. "And do you favor one of them?" I said that I did. "Then do it. Do it." He paused.

"But remember, just remember. A job is only a platform. And all platforms are made of wood. Sooner or later they rot. You were born into this world for only one reason: to serve God."

A longer pause. There's not much to say after such a pronouncement. Dick broke the silence. "Say," he said, "I better get this stuff to Albuquerque by noon, or I'll lose the contract."

71

I closed the truck door, and Dick began to drive away. As he went, he shouted out his window," Excuse me for minding your business. You were born into this world for only one reason: to serve God."

His final words reminded me of the words of John Henry Newman: "Never less alone than when alone." In that moment, all alone, I was fully surrounded by God's presence and, right then and there, a whole new life began for me. It was Easter.

Chapter Five

DIRECT AND RULE OUR HEARTS

The season of Pentecost offers twenty-nine different collects drawn from a variety of sources. Speaking in a range of voices, each collect touches on different issues we all face and allows us to open our hearts to God. The season of Pentecost is often called ordinary time. Here are reflections on five of the collects for Pentecost that point to and underscore the reality of ordinary time.

O Lord, mercifully receive the prayers of your people who call upon you, and grant that they may know and understand what things they ought to do, and also may have grace and power faithfully to accomplish them; through Jesus Christ our Lord, who lives and reigns with you and the Holy Spirit, one God, for ever and ever. Amen.   (Proper 10, 231)

THE SUMMER OF MY TWENTIETH BIRTHDAY I traveled with my family throughout Europe. As it turned out, this was the last extended period of time I would spend with my parents. Many memories of our conversations remain, but much time was spent alone. Deeply in love, throughout long stretches of that summer all I did was dream about the person I loved, who was far away, spending time with new friends, among whom she discovered a new love interest. Those days far from her were exquisite torture.

Half of the summer was spent in England, a full week in The Lygon Arms, a grand old hotel in the small village of Broadway. Arriving on a Saturday, the following Sunday morning we attended the village church. The collect appointed contained similar petitions and struck deep chords for me. Throughout the following week, more than once a day, I returned to the small stone church to pray in silence, repeating the collect. I realized I was never alone.

As I repeated the words of the collect over and over, what I wanted to know was if I could turn my life over to God and live according to God's will, would all be well? Nothing about those hours was easy. They were not magical, but as I prayed, the collect became a series of questions: *Would God receive my prayers as I called out in pain and need?* The fact that I had chosen to pray in a remote and quiet space designed for worship meant that God was surely present. But would God receive my prayers?

SHE HAD GIVEN UP attending Sunday services. The small country church was directly across the street from where she had lived for fifty years, but it had ceased to be a part of her life.

When her daughter fell seriously ill, there was no way she could travel to see her. In loneliness and despair, she crossed the street and sat in silence in the church.

The sun had risen, and the light—red, blue and gold—played across the walls of the chancel. She stared for a long time at the cross and the window depicting Jesus standing, knocking on the door. She wondered if anyone had let him come in.

With no forethought, she spoke. "Well, here I am. But where are you?"

The response was strong and clear. "I'm right here with you."

No voice echoed through St. Matthew's Church in Broadway, England, on the days I sat there, all alone, but God's presence was powerful, and God's response was sure.

Would God grant me to know and understand what things I ought to do?

There were several options. In the silence and in the words of the collect, it became clear that the choice of vocation and the choice a life's companion were closely related, bound up one with the other.

The person with whom I would spend my entire life and the work that best expressed what God had given me to do were parts of a whole. There were neither voices nor signs, or were there? As I sat in silence and repeated the words— "Lord, be open to the prayers of thy humble servants; and that they may obtain their petitions make them to ask such things as shall please thee" — my conviction grew and has not left me.

When we drove out of Broadway at the end of the week, I knew more about the things I ought to do than when we had arrived. *Would God give me the grace and power faithfully to accomplish them?*

One knows the answer to this question only at the very end of life. There is nothing else to do but launch forth, set sights, get going. Grace and power will be provided. You are not alone; you are never alone. Grace is undeserved. All power comes from God, who will not leave us comfortless. God offers strength and assurance.

Where is prayer in all of this? Prayer is the practice of the presence of God. Prayer is the channel, the means, and the avenue through which God enters our life and surrounds us with grace and power.

Almighty God, the fountain of all wisdom, you know our necessities before we ask and our ignorance in asking: Have compassion on our weakness, and mercifully give us those things which for our unworthiness we dare not, and for our blindness we cannot ask; through the worthiness of your Son Jesus Christ our Lord, who lives and reigns with you and the Holy Spirit, one God, now and for ever. Amen. (Proper 11, 231)

As I was sitting, talking and drinking coffee with a friend one morning, his infant son came crawling into his father's study. The baby looked up, saw the fireplace screen and implements, increased speed and headed right for them. It was evident that after reaching his goal he would try to pull himself up on the fire screen, which would not hold him. He would fall backward, be hit by the screen, no doubt be hurt, and cry.

While wanting to intercept the child, something told me this was none of my business. I deliberately sat on my hands. Neither my friend nor I spoke. The little boy kept moving, determined, and the scene unfolded exactly as I anticipated. As the boy lay bawling on the floor, his father rescued and comforted his son, saying, "We both knew exactly what was going to happen. Better to let it unfold, as it should. That way he'll learn."

An undignified comparison, but the point is that God knows our necessities before we ask. God is the fountain of all wisdom. God is God, and while every description of God is beyond all analogies, God is omniscient, omnipresent, and all-powerful. When we enter the presence of God in prayer, we enter a realm unlike any we have ever known and completely beyond our comprehension. Nonetheless, one thing we do know: God is aware of our necessities before we ask and our ignorance in asking.

So why ask? The answer is found, among other places, in the story of blind Bartimaeus in Mark 10:46–52:

They came to Jericho. As he and his disciples and a large crowd were leaving Jericho, Bartimaeus son of Timaeus, a blind beggar, was sitting by the roadside. When he heard that it was Jesus of Nazareth, he began to shout out and say, "Jesus, Son of David, have mercy on me!" Many sternly ordered him to be quiet, but he cried out even more loudly, "Son of David, have mercy on me!" Jesus stood still and said, "Call him here." And they called the blind man, saying to him, "Take heart; get up, he is calling you." So throwing off his cloak, he sprang up and came to Jesus. Then Jesus said to him, "What do you want me to do for you?" The blind man said to him, "My teacher, let me see again." Jesus said to him, "Go; your faith has made you well." Immediately he regained his sight and followed him on the way.

"What do you want me to do for you?" Jesus knew what Bartimaeus wanted, just as God knows our necessities before we ask, but the fact remains that it is necessary that we state what it is that brings us into the presence of God.

"What do you want me to do for you?" God knows. But do we? Are we absolutely sure? If we are to be sure, if we are to know, then we must shape the words, ask the question, make the request.

THEY HAD BEEN MARRIED more than three years and desperately wanted to have children. Every kind of test and the best medical help could not determine any reason for infertility. They believed they should be parents; they wanted to be parents; they were prepared to be parents, but they were not parents. Parenthood should have happened long ago. Only it didn't.

The time had come to accept reality. For reasons they could not understand nor explain they would never be parents. The time had come to sit down, look each other in the eye, and tell the truth, but they just could not bring themselves to say the words.

Instead, they discussed other alternatives: foster parenthood and adoption. But there was no clear, definite reason for these choices—yet. The operative question had still not been framed or spoken. Before they could move forward they needed to say the words, to state the reality.

It finally happened one night at the dinner table. Wednesday evening, sitting at opposite ends of the table, feeling as if they were yards from one another, it was her turn to say grace. She said it. "Bless this food to our use and us to thy faithful and loving servants, and, if it is thy will—please make it your will—may we become parents of your beloved child, through Jesus Christ, our Lord. Amen."

Finally, they had prayed the words, told God, right out loud they wanted to have a child. As they ate the lamb stew, made from her mother's recipe, there were more tears than talk. At the very next conceivable moment, she became pregnant.

Will it always happen? Will God answer the question precisely as we wish? Of course not. But we need first to immerse ourselves in the practice of prayer, knowing at least one thing: God will have compassion on our weakness, for our weakness is so vast, so deep, so pervasive. Of this there is no doubt, and this we must acknowledge.

"For lo, between our sins and their reward, We set the passion of thy Son our Lord." In prayer we ask God to *give us those things which for our unworthiness we dare not, and for our blindness we cannot, ask.* We do so through the worthiness of Jesus Christ. We may not know what is best for us, and we do not deserve even to ask for anything at all. God in graciousness and mercy will be present with us in prayer for one reason and one reason only — Jesus Christ.

O God, because without you we are not able to please you, mercifully grant that your Holy Spirit may in all things direct and rule our hearts; through Jesus Christ our Lord, who lives and reigns with you and the Holy Spirit, one God, now and for ever. Amen.

(Proper 19, 233)

This is one of the shortest and simplest of all the collects to be found in The Book of Common Prayer. It may also say far more than most. Prayer, the practice of the presence of God, requires one thing above all else for us to undertake it: God's presence with us and in our lives, our every thought and action. Prayer only begins when we invite God into our lives. God who made us will not intrude. God is everywhere. God is always with us, but God's presence does not become real and evident unless and until we ask God to be present with us in each given moment.

This collect is so very relevant to every single moment and event. It describes where and how prayer begins. Once prayer begins then it will continue, as God's Holy Spirit invades and surrounds us, directing and ruling all that we do and say and ask. It is the simplest thing in the world — and the most difficult.

Jesus prayed in the garden of Gethsemane the night before he died: "Abba, Father, for you all things are possible; remove this cup from me; yet, not what I want but what you want." We can do the same.

IT WAS THE MOST DIFFICULT THING he'd ever faced. The night before, he couldn't eat, had no appetite, knew he shouldn't have a drink. He had to be at his best, his very best. This was a test.

They went to bed early. She watched television. He had no interest, but try as he might — and he did try — nothing brought the peace of sleep. He tossed and turned. She offered to rub his back. Her strokes became slower and slower. Knowing she was drifting off to sleep, he reached over, found the control, turned off the TV and then her reading light.

Now he was flat in the bed, staring up, up into the darkness in the direction of where heaven was supposed to be, if there were such a place, even such an idea.

As the sound of her measured breathing became more evident, he envied her ability to find peace and rest. All he knew right now was anxiety. He thought of getting up, getting out, walking the streets. What for? Perhaps sleep would come.

Everything was in readiness. No preparation had been forgotten. He had done all the things he ought to have done, but he wished, how he wished, that he could advance the clock by twenty-four hours and have it all behind him.

He tried counting, tried imagining this exact day a year ago, wondered where their children were right now. Nothing worked. The coming morning kept haunting him. He decided to do the impossible: face into it, create the worst possible scenario—live with it, then live through it. He did. It worked.

As he began to drop off to sleep, he started to pray: "Our Father, who art in heaven, hallowed be thy Name...." The next thing he knew the alarm sounded.

Almighty and everlasting God, you are always more ready to hear than we to pray, and to give more than we either desire or deserve: Pour upon us the abundance of your mercy, forgiving us those things of which our conscience is afraid, and giving us those good things for which we are not worthy to ask, except through the merits and mediation of Jesus Christ our Savior; who lives and reigns with you and the Holy Spirit, one God, for ever and ever. Amen. (Proper 22, 234)

Prayer is a process, a way of life that leads us on, hour by hour, day by day, year by year. It is powered by God's presence. Prayer is God's presence.

AS THEY STARTED OUT from the city to drive one hundred miles into the country to spend the weekend with family, the snow had just begun to fall. Nothing serious; they were to travel on main roads. Forty-five minutes later the snow was very heavy and accumulating rapidly. There were no signs of salt trucks or plows.

The accident happened at the same time it first occurred to him to be worried. Rounding a great wide curve and traveling at a very reasonable rate of speed, the rental car, with no warning, lost all traction, swerved, as if on its own, to the right and into the roadside ditch, pitched wildly, reversed direction, almost rolled over and came to rest. The motor was still running, the car completely immobile.

"Are you all right?" she screamed, as he said the exact same words. Stunned, no one spoke further; each cried. The driver's side of the car was buried in the ditch. Then, just as he had said, "See if you can open your door" it opened by itself, a hand reached in and a voice said, "Is everything all right? Any one hurt?"

"We're fine," they both said. "But we can't get out!"

"Give me your hand," the voice replied, "and I'll help you out." Soon they were both standing on the bank. "You had quite a scare," said the Good Samaritan. Actually there were two Good Samaritans, their car idling on the road above. The driver was younger — in his twenties. The man who had come first to their aid was ten or more years his senior. Both voices were marked by regional accents.

"We've placed a call to the State Police. There's a trooper only a mile away. He'll be here soon and will call for a tow."

The rescue proceeded as predicted: the trooper arrived, called for a tow, and invited the two victims to sit in his cruiser. "Just don't touch any of those buttons and don't drive away," he said with a smile. Photographs of his wife and two young children were attached to the sun visor.

Once their car was righted and back on the road, the trooper bid them farewell. As they got into the car and settled down, the older of their two rescuers, who had done most of the talking and was clearly the one in charge, approached them for one final time. "So where are you headed?" he asked. They told him. "Look," he went on, "we're headed that way. Follow us, at least for the next thirty or so miles. You must be shaken up. An escort will do you good."

Although their thanks had been profuse from the first time his hand had reached into their car, now they got out of the car to shake hands and ask where the two men lived. The older man never gave his name or address, but they discovered that the younger lived just blocks from their old house. Fifteen years had passed since they had lived there, but the coincidence was overwhelming.

"How can we ever thank you?" the travelers asked.

"Think nothing of it. The fact you're alive and well is more than enough thanks. We're just glad that we were here to help. Come along now, get in your car and follow us."

They did as bidden. Thirty miles down the road, the rescuers turned left with a wave and a honk. The adventure was over, or at least the first part of it. After the visit with family ended, they drove back to the city and flew home. Neither could stop reflecting aloud about their remarkable experience. A greater expression of thanks was required. They telephoned a friend who lived in their old neighborhood and asked if he would make a personal call, contact the two men, both the younger and the older, and offer two Super Bowl tickets — a perfect present.

The day after their call, the phone rang soon after eight in the morning. Their old neighborhood friend said, "If you're not sitting down, please do. I did what you asked, and what I discovered you'll not believe.'

"What is it?"

"Remember that little neighborhood convenience store?"

"Sure, it was nothing but trouble. We never allowed our students to go near the place."

"Right. And remember one night two boys went into that store, one seventeen and the other his little brother. The older was stoned and tried to hold up the place. The clerk resisted; the older kid stabbed him with a knife, spent the next twelve years in prison but was released because he'd committed the crime as a juvenile. Well, that's the guy who saved you when you went into the ditch."

Coincidence is God's way of remaining anonymous. Be assured of one thing, the God who is present will give more than we either desire or deserve.

The God who was present on that day and throughout the lives of all those involved was present for and with everyone of them, forgiving us those things of which our conscience is afraid and giving us those good things for which we are not worthy to ask, except through the merits and mediation of Jesus Christ our Savior.

 Blessed Lord, who caused all holy Scriptures to be written for our learning: Grant us so to hear them, read, mark, learn, and inwardly digest them, that we may embrace and ever hold fast the blessed hope of everlasting life, which you have given us in our Savior Jesus Christ; who lives and reigns with you and the Holy Spirit, one God, for ever and ever. Amen. (Proper 28, 236)

The collect instructs and reminds us of the importance of repeated reflection on the words of Holy Scripture. There are many ways to engage Scripture, different practices to make it part of daily life. One prominent way in the Anglican tradition is reading the Daily Office, in solitude, in an informal group, or in the nave of a parish church.

We had gathered with old friends for a few days of conversation and renewal of friendship in a small inn on the coast of Maine. After breakfast on the first day, we sat in the sun, drinking coffee. Someone suggested that we read the Daily Office. A prayer book and Bible were located, and we began, using the assigned lessons. We had no idea what they would be. They were Psalm 80, Judges 6:25–40, Acts 2:37–47, and John 1:1–18. These are "Hear, O Shepherd of Israel, leading Joseph like a flock," a landmark story of

Gideon, the original definition of the apostolic fellowship to which we all belong, and the prologue to the Gospel according to John.

When the lessons had been read, the prayers spoken and the Office concluded, the four sat in silence for some time. The first reaction was to reflect on the power of the lessons, chosen in sequence for this Monday in August. Surely the lessons for this particular day were unusual, but the amazing fact is that the Daily Office lectionary for each and every day of the year will contain such treasures.

It is not necessary to affirm that the Holy Scriptures are a treasure house of insight, wisdom, inspiration and new insight, but on that morning the four of us learned how much each of us benefits by reading and reflecting on the Scripture assigned to the day.

In the long oblong blur we call the past, those few moments in the morning sun with dear and old friends stand out.

Each Tuesday morning during my years on the faculty of Virginia Seminary eleven advisees appeared in my living room to sit in a circle and read the Daily Office, pray, and talk. As the discipline was engrained in each of us, this became the best hour of the week. The personal engagement with the passages of Scripture and the opportunity to pray together changed us. A great deal happened as we engaged Scripture and one another; we grew. It was not always easy, but it was sure. We moved together.

Membership changed each year. My final year there could not have been greater variety. Age, background, theological, and political perspectives embraced a wide spectrum. There was little agreement on any matter, save the importance of what we were about each Tuesday morning.

The Seminary's tradition was to change the composition of advisee groups each year. This group petitioned the Dean, and she granted the request, that they be allowed to stay together throughout their three years as students.

Why did this group, so disparate, find unity? Prayer was the prevailing reason. The context was established by Scripture that created the discipline of praying together for common concerns in the name of one Lord.

The collect asks us not only to read, mark, learn, and inwardly digest all Holy Scripture, but also to embrace and hold fast the blessed hope of everlasting life.

Each day of our life is lived in a framework. That framework is created by the meaning of twin realities: time and death. Where does it all begin and end? Is this all there is? What does it all mean? What's next?

Our eleven-year-old grandson experienced a great loss: the death of the fifty-year-old father of his classmate and friend. After dinner on a Tuesday evening, the friend's father stretched out on the living room couch to watch the evening news. He fell asleep. At ten o'clock when his wife came to wake him, she found that he was dead. What happens now? Is there more? There is everlasting life, but for our grandson, there are questions.

The point is that those who believe in our Savior Jesus Christ have an answer. The answer is everlasting life that God has given us in our Savior Jesus Christ; who lives and reigns with you and the Holy Spirit, one God, for ever and ever.

Chapter Six

INESTIMABLE LOVE

During my years in grade school, summers were spent on Squam Lake in New Hampshire. A boy who was exactly my age became a close friend. Matt and I loved to fish and hunted the frogs we used for bait, catching them with our bare hands, while wading in the water at the end of a dark, grassy cove called The Bight.

When Matt and I were twelve, his mother and father divorced. As the much younger child of the family, Matt chose to become a Roman Catholic like his mother, and he left the Episcopal Church. There was at that time a great divide in Boston, where I grew up, between those who were Roman Catholics and those who were not. Matt was the very first Roman Catholic I had ever known, and also one of my few friends who took religious commitment seriously. He actually believed that prayer was important. He was also the only male friend with whom I corresponded regularly as we each grew up and attended different boarding schools.

Matt's school experience was quite different from mine. After he became a Roman Catholic, first he chose to attend a strict Roman Catholic boarding school, and after only a year, decided to study for the Roman Catholic priesthood and entered St. Charles Seminary in Baltimore. When I visited him there, I met the rector and attended the Veneration of the Blessed Sacrament. I saw the consecrated communion bread held aloft, encased in the center of a large round gold monstrance. It was different from anything I had ever known.

My father was very fond of Matt and never tired of talking with him about his theological interests and his career. My father's success in Boston was rooted in part in his ability to understand and talk meaningfully with serious Roman Catholics. During Matt's visit I discovered my father knew far more about these things than I did. He was emphatic, for instance, that Matt undertake his final years in seminary in Innsbruck, Austria, and study under Josef Jungmann, an outstanding liturgical scholar. Matt did so. He went on to translate Jungmann's definitive work on the Roman Catholic Mass and became a distinguished liturgical scholar.

On this occasion, however, well before his years in Innsbruck, Matt and I would talk about The Book of Common Prayer, its words and cadences, the majesty and simplicity of language that had the ability to focus our lives in prayer. The parts of Morning Prayer we held in common and had so often celebrated together, especially The General Thanksgiving, captured us.

✠ Almighty God, Father of all mercies,
    we thine unworthy servants
do give thee most humble and hearty thanks
for all thy goodness and loving-kindness
to us and to all men.
We bless thee for our creation, preservation,
and all the blessings of this life;
but above all for thine *inestimable* love
in the redemption of the world by our Lord Jesus Christ,
for the means of grace, and for the hope of glory.
And, we beseech thee,
give us that due sense of all thy mercies,
that our hearts may be *unfeignedly* thankful;
and that we show forth thy praise,
not only with our lips, but in our lives,
by giving up our selves to thy service,
and by walking before thee
in holiness and righteousness all our days;
through Jesus Christ our Lord,
to whom, with thee and the Holy Ghost,
be honor and glory, world without end. Amen.

(BCP, 58–29; emphasis added)

Two words — *inestimable* and *unfeignedly* — became the centerpiece of our discussion. Their use was emphasized on Sunday when we attended Trinity Church, Boston, to hear Theodore Parker Ferris preach. The nave was so full that Matt and I could not sit together. He was seated several pews in front of me, and to my right. When the time came to recite The General Thanksgiving in unison, as we said the words *inestimable* and then *unfeignedly,* my friend raised and turned his head to look at me and smile.

What his glance and smile said to me is this: these two words may be cumbersome, unwieldy and seldom used, but they are the two most essential words in this very old, important prayer. The roots of this General Thanksgiving are found in words written in 1596 as the beginning of the phrasing of a thanksgiving to be used as a private prayer of Queen Elizabeth I. This phrasing suggested the word *inestimable* to describe God's love on our behalf. What better word could there be?

The act of thanksgiving is an essential part of all of life, most especially the Christian life. Our life is rooted in thanksgiving, the recognition that all life flows from God, and we live and breathe and have our being in God. Prayer is grounded in thanksgiving, the acknowledgement that God — the source of all there was, or is, or ever will be — gave his very life to us and for us in Christ. God in Christ made the ultimate sacrifice on our behalf so that we may not only live, day by day, but find our lives constantly renewed. This gift is inestimable.

The word *inestimable* is seldom heard and little understood today. It means too precious to be estimated, priceless, too great, too profound or intense to be estimated. In the twenty-first century, inestimable is a foreign concept. In our world everything has a cost and a price. One's worth is measured in dollars and cents. Possessions have a very definite market value that may be measured. Totals are added together, conclusions drawn, agreements reached.

More is better. How much is enough? There is never enough. But the measurement, the figuring, the acquisition continues. We never escape it.

Consider the casual question: "How far is it from here to New York City?" The answer will probably be, "Oh, it's about two hours."

The question asked for a particular distance, something measurable, a hundred miles. The number of miles to New York could have been easily supplied, but instead, the answer will almost always be given in time. Time is a proper currency. Time is money. Time has measurable value; however, it is not inestimable. There is only so much of it. We can relate to that. Inestimable is of a completely different order.

Money should be the same as time: finite, definite, limited. Only we think we can extend these limits. We borrow. The United States Government does it. Not just the liberal spenders, who want everything for everyone, but now, even the most hidebound conservatives. It's called running up the debt. Living beyond our limits. Everyone does it, but if we do, there are consequences. One way or another, we have to pay for what we spend. We live in a world of limits.

This is not the case in the world created for us that is defined by God's love. God and God's love are inestimable, and therefore beyond all measure and comparison.

HE WAS A MAN from another time, another age. A rector in downtown Atlanta in the years just before the *Brown v. Board of Education* decision of the Supreme Court in 1954. Peter was tall, carefully and deliberately spoken, prematurely bald, courtly. He was also ahead of his time. He was socially active, progressive one might say, decidedly liberal, a man who believed that the Christian Gospel and the presence of God in Christ were rooted in freedom, given to each and every one of us so that we might become more the persons we were created by God to be.

In 1952 Peter had committed his energies and the program of his church to move the equality and integration of black people and white people forward. On one particular Sunday, he announced that the NAACP would hold a meeting on Tuesday evening in the parish hall to which all were invited. The sermon that day spoke of God's will for God's people of all races. It was a strong and eloquent statement. Peter believed it and lived it with all of his being.

When the service concluded, one man hung back, waiting to speak to the rector after all the other parishioners had made their way out of the door. The gentleman, equipped with hat and gloves carried in his left hand, limped, held a black ebony cane in his right hand, and wore a morning coat. When he reached the rector, he began with neither greeting nor handshake, only these words:

"If I am ever again present in this parish church, where my family has belonged for one hundred and thirty-two years, and hear such a sermon preached or announcements about Negroes being welcome to use this property, I shall cancel my pledge and never return. Never. Do you understand, sir?"

He paused, to let his message sink in, and then he continued, "And should it have slipped your mind, Rector, may I remind you that my pledge is five thousand dollars per year."

That was all. The gentleman donned his hat, slid on one of his gloves and began to make his way out the door. He stopped, however, and turned back to look at the rector when Peter finally spoke. "I'm sure every man has his price," he said. "I am even sure that I have my price. But it certainly isn't a lousy five thousand dollars."

Inestimable. Some things are beyond value and beyond all counting. Jesus spoke of the pearl of great price, the love of a father for a wayward son, the widow's mite, the lost sheep. His language was rich in metaphor, asking hearers and followers to stretch their minds beyond the humdrum and the ordinary, to know that his world, Jesus' world, God's world, was different from the daily and the humdrum. God's world is beyond measure: inestimable.

Jesus was not a bean counter. He spoke of and created a kingdom where the goodness and the potential of life were beyond calculation. The love of God, expressed through Christ to all God's people, all of God's creation, is beyond estimate and measure. What he knew and asked us to understand was inestimable. What does this mean when we pray? Prayer allows us to enter a different dimension, a dimension beyond measurement that stretches into all dimensions, into all of space at one and the same time. When we pray we open our hearts, reveal our secrets, make ourselves accessible to God. We come closer to the love that is inestimable, known in no other context, but available to everyone of us.

And how do we respond to the inestimable? *Unfeignedly.* We are unfeignedly thankful, and, again, enter a realm virtually unknown.

This word, too, is seldom used. We have no use for it. *Unfeignedly* describes a world in which there are no secrets — none — hidden or revealed. *Unfeignedly* describes the state in which we are totally genuine, open, honest, and sincere, a condition we seldom experience. It is the condition I first discovered when I fell in love. It describes the way I felt as I entered surgery, when the outcome was uncertain.

The General Thanksgiving states that we are unfeignedly thankful, because God's love that has been offered to us and received by us is inestimable.

The knowing gaze that my friend Matt turned on me that Sunday morning said, "Pay attention. You and I should pay attention. We have just heard an ineffable, heretofore unknown, miracle described." God so loved the world that he gave his only begotten Son. God's inestimable love has been given to us, and in return, we are unfeignedly thankful.

This is something that has never happened before or since. It is incomparable, beyond all estimation and our wildest imagination. It is ours, here and now, through the means and the grace and the possibility of prayer.

When moments that we welcome and celebrate happen, what do we do? We pray. Prayer is possible because God's love is inestimable. In the presence of this love we are unfeignedly thankful.

Chapter Seven

UNTO WHOM ALL HEARTS
ARE OPEN

The Holy Eucharist is a corporate act requiring that two or three or more be gathered around the Lord's table and invoke his presence, his body and blood in the bread and the wine. Why then turn to the Holy Eucharist as a resource for private prayer?

A prayer I use often when alone in the presence of God is this:

Be present, be present, O Jesus, our great High Priest, as you were present with your disciples, and be known to us in the breaking of bread; who live and reign with the Father and the Holy Spirit, now and forever. Amen. (BCP, 834)

The presence of Christ made clear in the Eucharist is not limited to specific moments brought to life in the words of consecration. The reality of Christ's presence evident in the bread and wine at that moment continues. Prayer is the practice of the presence of God. An essential part of this presence that comes to us in the Eucharist continues to be part of our daily lives in the hours and days that follow the celebration of the Holy Eucharist.

> **Almighty God, unto whom all hearts are open, all desires known, and from whom no secrets are hid: Cleanse the thoughts of our hearts by the inspiration of thy Holy Spirit, that we may perfectly love thee, and worthily magnify thy holy Name; through Christ our Lord. Amen.**
>
> (The Collect for Purity, 323)

This collect begins with an astounding statement. If it were not completely true, it would be unbelievable. As we prepare to enter the presence of God, these words announce that we come to a place where we may be completely and utterly honest. It sets the tone that pervades the Holy Eucharist, the central act of Christian corporate worship. Here is a special dimension that defines the moment when we open our lives to God in prayer. Since there are so very few occasions in any lifetime when this is true, what might it be like?

After my eleven-year-old grandson experienced the death of his friend's father, his mother told me how he was coping.

"Last night Matthew came to me and told me that he could not sleep. He was too sad. As we lay there together in the dark, the tears began to fall. His tears were gut-wrenching, tears of such sadness, empathy and compassion for his friend. They were tears of love and concern, tears of deep pain and loss and grief. As I lay beside him, my own tears streaming, I stroked his back and struggled to find the words to comfort him.

"While Matthew wept for his friend Will and all that Will had lost, between sobs, he began to describe all the love he saw between Will and his father. He spoke of all the things they loved to do together, how present the father had been in Will's life and how much Will loved and respected his father. It was then that I thought, 'Matthew is only eleven, but he sees and speaks what is true. The boy knows love when he sees it.'

"We talked and cried and wondered how this could happen. Why? Why? Why? 'What will Will do?' Matthew asked over and over. There were no answers. The finality of the reality of death enfolded us.

"For the first time as Matthew's mother, I did not have an answer to take away the sadness. Then I said what I believe. 'God is here, God is speaking to you in your tears of love and compassion. Yes, Will's father is gone, but the love is not gone. Nothing can take away the love they had.' "

"After a long silence, Matthew said, 'I'm feeling more peaceful.'

" 'Why?' I asked.

" 'Because the love will always be there. Always. It can never die. Nothing can take that away from Will. Will is going to be all right.' "

There are moments — rare, unexpected, welcome and unwelcome — when we know that *hearts are open, desires known, and...no secrets are hid.* These are the moments when God is present. These are moments of prayer.

SEVEN OF THEM, all women, met at two o'clock on the first Wednesday of every month. No one referred to it as a prayer group, although each knew why she had come.

Martha, who convened the group, was ninety, virtually blind, and now lived alone since the death of her husband two years ago. Their first son had died in World War II, and when the second son was born, they gave him the same name. She was washing the breakfast dishes the day two Marines arrived at the door to tell them he'd been killed in Vietnam.

The other members of the group ranged in age from thirty to eighty-five. Not all knew each other beyond this gathering, but the bands of connection and affection were strong in the circle in which they sat. Without preparation or assignment, each month one or more brought a thought, a poem, a prayer for consideration at the opening.

For the next two hours each spoke in turn of what mattered most, what she had taken seriously without any consideration in the days since they had last met. Topics discussed covered a wide range. Each was presented with honesty and deep feeling.

Problems did find solutions, but more important was the fact that concerns were heard with compassion and understanding.

Before they rose to leave at four o'clock, Martha would ask that they hold hands while she spoke words of prayer. But of course all the words spoken in that circle had been prayer. When these women gathered they opened their hearts and spoke to one another only of what was most important. All secrets were left outside the front door and never entered the room.

Far too often virtually the entire time of our life, the opposite is true. Individuals and the entire world are defined by secrets. These secrets are the things we deliberately do not say, things we keep to ourselves and do not reveal.

The whole world of marketing is based on the premise that we need to tell people what they want to hear, not what is actually the truth. Describe the product that people want, and they will buy. The art of dissembling is richly rewarded.

The closer people live together, the more intimate the group, the less likely this is to be true. During several years of association with independent schools, I frequently said that a school *can* be more like a parish than any parish I have known. When I made such a statement, many replied they did not understand what I meant. One reason for this misunderstanding is that when an independent school functions well, it is a place where people live and work together closely. They know one another's business, and they mind one another's business. Is the result perfect? No, but there is the opportunity for hearts to be open, desires known, and no secrets hid.

In a perfect world there are no secrets; there is no need for secrets. Each of the sixteen years I served as headmaster I assigned myself the faculty responsibility of overseeing one of the six classes, which meant that I met with them, as a whole class, once each week. One year many new students had been admitted to the ninth grade, for which I was responsible. They were on the cusp of adolescence, brash, new, full of that strange mixture of uncertainty and bravado. I thought I should tell them about the nature of this small, enclosed community. So one Tuesday, early in the year, I remember saying to them, "You may well choose not to believe me, but I want to tell you, especially those of you who are new, something unusual about this school. People know pretty much everything about everyone else. None more so than the headmaster. For some reason that I do not completely understand, sooner or later, I get to know all there is to know. So be careful. This doesn't mean I can behave as if I knew everything, but it still remains true that I'll know. If you think there are secrets, there are. Only they are never secrets for very long."

What I said next was one of the worst examples of telling boys and girls not to put beans up their nose. I actually went on to say, "Why. today, for instance, this very morning, if one of you has a free period and goes down behind the tennis courts and smokes, by about 2:30, when the school breaks from classes and goes to sports, some faculty member will stop by my office and tell me exactly what happened." I paused and looked around at forty boys and girls. They were listening but, I wondered, Did they hear?

At 2:45 p.m. that very afternoon, a member of the faculty stopped by to tell me that he had seen — not caught — a new member of the ninth grade, smoking down behind the tennis courts.

Yes, there were secrets in that community, many of them hidden, but most often not for long and not hidden from the headmaster, who, for some reason, was trusted enough to be told most things about most other people. But how was I to act? Often, I did. No doubt not enough, and the burden that remained was great. I knew about faculty marriages and parent marriages that were collapsing — the fact hidden from common knowledge. I knew of students who lived in households where the alcohol abuse was unbearable and repressive. I was well aware that older boys in the twelfth grade preyed on the insecure younger girls. And I knew far too much about the unhappy little boy who stole from others in his dormitory but would never be caught. This was the same boy whose parents asked me to be the one to tell him first that they were to be divorced, and his life would change forever. Like a fool, I did just that, and the boy never spoke to me again, not until the moment I handed him his diploma, and he said, "Thank you."

Much of my time, too often while lying in bed late at night unable to sleep, I struggled with what to do with this knowledge — the reality that I lived in a world where most secrets were not hid, but known, at least by me. Yet, there was too often little or nothing that I could do, save for the few times I could anticipate the inevitable and head it off before it became unmanageable.

We live in an imperfect world, a world full of the unexpected, a world of surprises and secrets. This is not the world that God created for you and for me. With God all hearts are open, all desires known, and from God no secrets are hid. And how does such a world become available to us? Through prayer. This collect sets the tone for this prayer and all of our prayer, all of it.

On Good Friday during our youngest daughter's senior year in college, since she attended a college not far from home, I proposed that she and her mother and I together attend the three-hour service at the University Church. Who knew what the future held for the three of us? This might be the very last time we could worship together at such a service, and, as it has happened, it was. Mother and daughter agreed.

Once the service began I became aware that there was very serious work being done beside me by both mother and daughter. Some will say that I'm just nosey, but in any case, as we walked away from the church that afternoon, glorying in the strong April sunshine, I asked, "Eliza, you were deep in prayer during much of that service. What were you praying about?"

Walking half a step ahead of me and not turning around, Eliza replied, "Dad, that's private."

Her prayer life was secret. Prayer knows nothing about secrets. Prayer means that nothing is hid from God. Eliza knew a great deal about prayer, and she prayed with diligence and power. Her prayer may be private, as certainly it is, but it was one time, one place, one conversation, in which no secrets were hid, for there were no secrets. None at all.

When secrets are hid, they hurt. When secrets are known, there is healing. This is where prayer begins.

Prayer continues to its purpose which is to *cleanse the thoughts of our hearts*. We tell our secrets. We open our hearts, hearts that are known. We confess our desires so that we may be cleansed. And we are.

The greatest discovery of my life came when I fell in love. It happened this way. Fourteen years old, soon to be fifteen, I arrived at our summer community later than usual to discover, almost immediately, that there was a new girl. She and her family had arrived for the very first time and for the entire summer. Nick and Peter, friends from our earliest years, pointed her out sunning herself on the hot flat rocks on the point across the cove from the Main Dock. We swam across, and I met Anne.

All through that summer and the next two summers we became best friends, told each other everything, really everything. When each summer ended, and we returned to boarding school, we wrote. Long letters. For some reason each of us saved them. Being fourteen, fifteen and sixteen is not always comfortable or a great deal of fun. Through those years, however, there was one person — and one was more than enough — to whom I could tell everything. Not only could I, but I actually did. One person knew about my insecurities and my fears, my ambitions, small successes and massive failures. One person was safe; she knew my secrets.

During most of three summers, often at night, we crept off into the dark of the woods and sat on pine needles beneath tall trees to talk and listen, listen and talk. We were not in love; or, to be more accurate, we were not in lust. We were friends, best friends, friends who trusted one another implicitly and completely, friends who knew everything about the other, and still remained friends.

Then near the end of the third summer, it happened. No one was more surprised than I when completely without warning, on a beautiful starlit night, out in the middle of the lake in a boat, all alone, one night, we kissed. And that was that. We were still friends, but now we were also in love, and we have been ever since.

Among other things, what I had learned was that there was nothing bad, nothing wrong, not even anything really embarrassing, about my secrets. Anne knew them all and loved me nonetheless. That's a cleansing experience, a healing experience. In fact it is a constantly renewable source of new life.

It took a while, since I'm a slow learner, to realize that my experience was a humble manifestation of what happened for every one of us when God became incarnate as Jesus Christ. God, who shared our life at every level, knows all that we know and experience. But God loves us still and all, forgives us, cleanses us. Secrets no longer matter, no longer exist. Secrets vanish, for this is the God from whom no secrets are hid. This is the very same God who is also available to us in prayer. This is the God who comes among us and lives as one of us — and loves us still and all.

This is where prayer begins to find its goal in the reality *that we may perfectly love thee*, which is to say that we love fully. The word *perfect* means "whole." Our love is complete, all that we can offer, for there are no secrets, our hearts are open, and we are completely honest.

Towards the known coast my fragile vessel reaches
To breach the space made wide by a tidal rush.
I stand watching through the storm, and now
    struggle
Through these waters for return.
This beach and calmed cove are the comfort of
All I expected: the smooth round boulders,
Named and sure, remain where I remember.
I could find them in blindness even.
Small stones, some of them flat for skipping, and
    piles
Of mussel shells worn violet by the salt.
My boat tethered and far enough from the rising
    tide,
I sit and feel the solid rock beneath me.
I'm worn by that storm I've weathered.

Filled expectations: coming home to find all remains

The same, yet different. The sea wall crumbled,
The roots of worried trees exposed to light, to wind.
Winter churned and changed this beach.
The sea returned what we had given it:
A shoe, a bottle, thought lost, have
Found their way here to hands, again.
If it all could be so easy, if what
We give freely might again return,
Like this smoothed blue glass, this pearled shell.
I gather them into my pocket, later to treasure.
I wish to gather back my heart, my unnamed hopes,
Lost like loon calls echoed across the bay.

 **The peace of the Lord be always with you.
And with thy spirit.** (The Peace, 332)

This ancient part of the Eucharist, originally known as the
Kiss of Peace, was restored to our liturgy in The Book
of Common Prayer (1979). Its practice varies widely. *The
peace of the Lord be always with you* pronounced at the
Sunday Parish Eucharist will sometimes provoke a lengthy
and enthusiastic fête of conversation. At an early morning celebration where most of those present are older
and unfamiliar with the Kiss of Peace, members of the
congregation will remain kneeling, deep in prayer.

When serving as chaplain in a non-church school, I
experimented with many forms of liturgy and on Easter
Day suggested something radical: the celebration of the
Eucharist. This had never happened before. The liturgy

we used was one written by W. H. Auden for St. Mark's Church In-the-Bowery in New York City and included the Kiss of Peace. In an all-boys residential school this possibility occasioned a long debate. All agreed that the Kiss of Peace meant that each person kissed another on the cheek, but this was not to be in a boys' boarding school.

So what should we do? Should we look one another in the eye, shake hands, exchange words of greeting, or grasp one another on the shoulder and say, "Good morning"? In the end each person did what he deemed best and most comfortable, but there was a clear understanding that this part of the liturgy called for honest exchange symbolizing our common brotherhood and unity. Such a serious moment was not to be feared and avoided nor turned into a wild moment of untamed emotion.

This part of the Eucharist reflects an essential reality about our life of prayer: its purpose is to relate us to others — both God in Christ and those persons who embody God's presence in our world. As we turn our attention toward the central action of the sacrament — The Great Thanksgiving and Words of Institution — we acknowledge our common bond in Christ that binds us one to another. This acknowledgment is prayer itself, and every time it happens it enriches prayer.

HER FOUR-YEAR-OLD GRANDDAUGHTER was gathering her possessions together, getting ready to climb into the car with her parents and sister to head home after spending the weekend with grandparents in the country. The moment was not welcome — parting is always a small death — but inevitable.

To ease the moment the little girl bent over and found a small, but nearly perfect oyster shell among the stones of the driveway. She stood, walked over to where her grandmother was standing talking to her mommy, held out her hand and the oyster shell, and said, "Here, Amah. Put this shell in a special place, and every time you see it, think of me and know that I am thinking of you."

She turned and climbed into her car seat, ready to go.

THE CLASS OF EIGHT was involved in an energetic discussion of marriage. Each member was married, each had strong opinions, and each was willing to enter the conversation fully and emphatically. It was not so much that there were different points of view but that every member was fully invested in the opportunity of marriage.

The conversation ranged wildly and for some time, finally reaching a crescendo of affirmation. Then, all of a sudden, there was complete and total silence. The teacher, sitting at the end of the table, allowed the silence to happen. After what seemed like several minutes, he said, "That was intercourse. Now we are spent. Let's take a break."

No one spoke as they filed out of the room.

The Peace of the Lord is not always present; moments such as these do not take place automatically or without effort. Whenever there is the opportunity to exchange the Peace of the Lord, whether in the context of the Eucharist, when two people meet, or within a group, if one person is excluded, even accidentally, the result is intense loneliness. God's presence in Christ is always a time to bind us together, one with another, but unless we extend the hand of fellowship in word or deed when the opportunity presents itself, then we deny another the communion offered in Christ.

God in Christ is ever present, but you and I are the ones who allow the Peace of the Lord to enter our midst.

Lift up your hearts.
We lift them up unto the Lord.
Let us give thanks unto our Lord God.
It is meet and right so to do.

It is very meet, right, and our bounden duty, that we should at all times, and in all places, give thanks unto thee, O Lord, holy Father, almighty, everlasting God. *Through Jesus Christ our Lord, who on the first day of the week overcame death and the grave, and by his glorious resurrection opened to us the way of everlasting life.* Therefore with Angels and Archangels, and with all the company of heaven, we laud and magnify thy glorious Name; evermore praising thee, and saying,

**Holy, holy, holy, Lord God of Hosts:
Heaven and earth are full of thy glory.
Glory be to thee, O Lord Most High.**

(*Sursum Corda* and *Sanctus*, 333–334, 345)

Therefore with Angels and Archangels, and with the company of heaven. In this instant of the fullness of time, in the very center of this particular liturgy, as we prepare for God to be present in this bread and this wine, we gather not just with the persons present around this altar, but with the great company of heaven. We ask God that, right now, as time and eternity intersect, to summon into our midst and in this moment the great company of heaven.

We are especially mindful of particular persons no longer living with whom we have knelt and stood together in the Eucharist — spouses, parents, siblings, mentors, colleagues, friends, and even enemies — the people who have marked our lives and made us who we are right now.

These people are here with us as at no other time in the week or the day or the year. We have come here to this time and place to be with them, to know and feel their presence, for they have been brought here to be with us, and we with them.

THE DAY HER HUSBAND DIED marked a new way of being alive. After forty-seven years of marriage, every conversation, decision and event of importance had been undertaken together. He had

114

been sick, but he had been sick before, and she never expected him to leave her with such short notice. He did. One moment he was there, talking, reflecting, thinking aloud, and then he was gone. Where once he had been, there was a corpse. She did not know what to do; she was beside herself.

After the Burial, when the friends had left and the children and grandchildren had gone home, and she was alone, she went to bed. She went under the covers of the great king-size expanse, where the two of them had slept and talked and made love. It was the only place where she felt comfortable, only she wasn't comfortable. She was lonely.

She stayed there more of each day than not, sometimes just lying on the top of the bed. She went out as little as possible, did not answer the phone, just wanted to be alone — with him. Only he was never there. He was dead.

Her daughter who lived a three-hour drive away came as often as she could, but given her life and professional responsibilities, those visits were never frequent enough or long enough. Doctors, counselors, and clergy listened and antidepressants helped for a few hours, until the effects wore off.

Since she stayed away from everyone and every place that reminded her of him, she didn't go to church, until early one Sunday morning when she felt compelled to show up in the pew where they had so often sat. And then she knew, she just knew, that he had come with her. Church had never been as important for him as for her, and he had often stayed at home Sunday morning reading the paper. Then, on the very day he died, he told her that he had seen God. She believed him.

God's presence in the Eucharist reunited them.

We do not presume to come to this thy Table, O merciful Lord, trusting in our own righteousness, but in thy manifold and great mercies. We are not worthy so much as to gather up the crumbs under thy Table. But thou art the same Lord whose property is always to have mercy. Grant us therefore, gracious Lord, so to eat the flesh of thy dear Son Jesus Christ, and to drink his blood, that we may evermore dwell in him, and he in us. Amen.

(Prayer of Humble Access, 337)

If we do not presume to trust in our own righteousness, then in whose righteousness do we trust? Every single one of us appears to be who we are not — to be the person we wish we could be, even though that is not who we are — and this is the very essence of being human. We want to be someone who feigns, a person who presumes to be who he or she is not.

When Thomas Cranmer wrote The Prayer of Humble Access (as the above prayer is known) in 1549, his goal was to describe the attitude of prayer that we adopt as we come forward to receive the bread and wine, the body and blood of Christ. Presumption has no place in this crucial moment that defines prayer. When we approach God in prayer, we do so without presumption.

Everyone has difficulty with this. To be genuine, honest and real is not the normal human stance. This is not the way that most of us were taught to greet the world. Snake oil salesmen were not merely a small, select band of Americans who helped open the Western frontier. They were not the only posers of that or any other time — persons who pretended to offer the world false solutions for many ills. Great fortunes are still won (and lost) by persons who deceive others. We *want* to appear behind a mask, we *want* to appear to be who we are not. The attitude of prayer is the complete opposite. Prayer does not presume.

Alcoholics Anonymous, whose business it is to help reclaim the lives of those who are addicted, starts with the understanding that there can be no pretense, no sham, no presumption, only the acknowledgment that each one of us is powerless. Once this is firmly and finally understood, new life is possible.

Prayer is a means to cut through all of this, a way to see the world not just the way we want to see it, but the way it is, the acknowledgement of God's presence. Whenever we stand before God, alone or with those we know and love the most, or in the midst of strangers, we are never alone. Christ is with us.

God knows
    I suppose
how our shadow slyly (or is it shyly?)
shows
what he'd hoped to
pose
as,

and so instead
God faces down
our fears for us

and shows our shadow to
the seeker
from whom we
fled,

and the prey we have
prayed we'd remain is instead
    ambushed
locked in the
ravishing embrace we knew all along would do us
in.

THIRTY YEARS after their high school graduation, more than half
the class gathered to celebrate common bonds and to know one
another anew. Events of the weekend centered on classmates
who spent their professional life making their gifts available to
others, rather than seeking their own financial gain. How could
they express what they took seriously without any reservation?
What was at the center of each life? What mattered more than
anything else?

"Is there anything that matters so much to you that you would
die for it? For what would you die?"

From the midst, a male voice replied, "I'd die for my partner. I
would die for John, who's sitting next to me."

There was a hush; the power of the testimony dumbfounding,
striking every one silent. The life-giving power was transforming.
Who among us does not wish that those words could be said of
us or for us?

AN AUNT OF MINE, well into retirement, visited one day every week in the male geriatric ward of a state mental hospital. For five years, every Tuesday morning, she greeted a man who sat in the far corner of the room in a catatonic state. He had been so totally and thoroughly hurt and crippled by the world that he had withdrawn from it entirely. He sat all day, day in, day out, in the same position, staring down at the floor, never responding, never acknowledging the presence of other persons, including my aunt, who spoke to him, again and again, each Tuesday for five years. There was never a response.

But Aunt Eleanor continued, always honest, never giving up, not welcoming but bearing the rejection. It was a Tuesday morning, like many others, when she greeted him once again with a "Good morning, Mr. Perkins. How are you this morning?" when he responded, "Quite well, thank you, Miss Richardson."

We may evermore dwell in him, and he in us. Our standing with God does not depend primarily on the things we do — good as they may be, helpful as they may be — but on what Christ has done for us. Somewhere, somehow we have been changed. We don't know how, but Christ has touched us and come into our lives, and we are no longer the same.

The Christian gospel is amazingly simple. What makes it hard to understand is that it is so different, so radically different, from normal day-to-day human experience that we have great difficulty understanding and appropriating it.

Prayer is the acknowledgement of God's presence. So too the reverse is true: when we acknowledge God's presence we are in prayer. It is no more complicated than that. Nor need it be. Moreover, when we acknowledge that we are not alone, but standing and living and breathing in the presence of God, who created and redeemed us and from whom all blessings flow, then new life is possible.

When we come forward to receive the body and blood of Christ, we are in an intensified attitude of prayer. This same attitude describes us at any and every time we enter the nearer presence of God to pray. The opportunity, that very moment, whenever and wherever it happens, is a gift. In this moment there are no demands, no restrictions, no expectations. One thing alone matters — that we offer ourselves, reveal ourselves, just as we are. We do not have to assume a role, complete any task, undertake any responsibility. We only have to be the person we have been created by God and intended to be.

But those moments, and others like them, all of them, opened life up in new ways. They opened the way to knowledge of God's presence, the assurance that God is always present. This is what it means that *we may evermore dwell in him, and he in us.*

✠ The peace of God, which passeth all understanding, keep your hearts and minds in the knowledge and love of God, and of his Son Jesus Christ our Lord; and

**the blessing of God Almighty, the Father, the Son, and the
Holy Ghost, be amongst you, and remain with you always.
Amen.** (The Blessing, 339)

This peace is the goal of our lives and of all our striving.
It's what we seek, what we crave, what we imagine. So we
are sent out from the altar of God into the world in search
of it. Or better still, we are sent out knowing that God's
peace will find us. It is not what we do, but what God in
Christ does in us and for us.

Peace strikes us. Peace breaks through. We never know
when it will happen, and it happens for each of us in different ways, at different times and in different places. Some
of these for me have been:

- That first moment I knew, really knew, I was in love.
- Making love and knowing we had conceived a child.
- Walking in the front door after a long absence.
- Being told we shall be parents.
- Looking at that child for the very first time.
- Walking down the aisle with that daughter.
- Asking for a gift of $50,000 and hearing the word,
  "Yes."
- Reading the letter announcing my first book would
  be published.

Those occasions came first to mind. Each announces
a beginning. Does peace always announce the first step

on a journey as one thinks of the past and remembers a single life-changing event? Does the peace that passes all understanding arrive only as a conclusion, or does it come to pass along the way?

The peace that passes all understanding occurs when we know, we just know, God is present. Whenever that happens, we are at prayer.

THE RENTAL CAR was not what he had specified. He should have just gotten in and driven away. Instead, he loaded the bags in the trunk, placed his briefcase behind the front seat and returned to the rental counter to complain. Julie was quick, efficient, more polite than he. The car he had just loaded was in space 112, and a new car, more to his liking, was in the very next space, 114. Paper work completed, they returned, opened the two trunks, transferred the bags, and departed.

The sun was bright, the traffic heavy. Ten miles down the four-lane highway, halfway to their destination, he said out loud, "Where's my briefcase? Where's my briefcase?" He reached around behind his seat to touch it resting in its accustomed place. It was not there. In one terrifying instant he realized he'd left it in the other car, no doubt now rented and driven away. Panic. The briefcase carried his small computer that contained everything he had written in the past fifteen years, including a book now in process, the text only in this computer.

Somehow they found the telephone number to the rental car office and then a space to cross the median strip — illegally — and they began the race back. He was desperate, hysterical. There was no hope. All was lost.

Her cell phone kept cutting out. Then the long recorded message, "Press five to change your reservation." Then a live, human voice. She explained. The response: "Someone will go and search the car." Dead air.

After an eternity, signs to the airport appeared. One turn, then another. He entered Rental Car Return searching for space 114. A man in a vest with HERTZ emblazoned on it waved them down, recognized hysteria, said, "Follow me." They did, pulled in next to 114, jumped out. There was the car! It was empty. Empty!

He ran into the small office, screaming, out of control. Julie was gone. The new agent, tall, statuesque, who thought much of herself, reprimanded him. Then out of the darkness, a tall, bald, young man appeared. "Here, follow me. We know what you're after. We have it." Unbelieving, he fell in behind him, as they strode across the garage to customer service. Inside the small space stood a man of medium height, wearing eyeglasses. His nametag read "Sanchez." Without a word, he opened a series of lockers. Nothing. When he opened the third one, there was the briefcase. "All I need to see is some identification."

"I could kiss you," said the briefcase owner.

"How about a handshake."

"You're wonderful, too wonderful. But who found it, who found it?"

"Ann Butler. She's inside."

The first woman he found behind the large interior counter wore a nametag that said, "Ann." He grabbed both of her hands. "You found it. You found it. I can never thank you enough. I'll write a letter to the Hertz office here and in Oklahoma City." She smiled.

He was so relieved and so drained he could scarcely make his way back to the car, but he was suffused by a sense of peace that passed all understanding. As far as he was concerned, it was a miracle.

And far more than that. Just moments before, he literally had thought that his life was about to come to an end. Everything he had accomplished in the past decade was contained in that small computer—a complicated little box—that now was gone. Life had been returned to him, and the peace he knew passed all understanding.

Keep your hearts and minds in the knowledge and love of God, and of his Son Jesus Christ our Lord. Prayer is not magic. It is the powerful assurance that we are filled and surrounded by the knowledge and the love of God.

Chapter Eight

HE LOVED THEM
TO THE END

✠ He stretched out his arms upon the cross, and offered himself, in obedience to your will, a perfect
sacrifice for the whole world. (Eucharistic Prayer A, 362)

These words describing the Eucharistic action are powerful and graphic, crucial to all we know and believe. We
are reminded that Jesus' suffering and death on our behalf
happened once and for all time, yet at the very same time
we here remember — make present in this moment — the
events of our salvation. The real presence of Jesus Christ
in our lives in the Eucharist does not occur once and for
all time in the past, but right here, right now.

This is not all, for this same transforming power and
presence are made present in our lives, through prayer.
Such prayer has many forms. One is the Jesus Prayer:

Lord Jesus Christ, Son of God, have mercy on me, a sinner.
Lord Jesus Christ, Son of God, have mercy on me, a sinner.
Lord Jesus Christ, Son of God, have mercy on me, a sinner.

Through hundreds of years, millions have discovered that praying these twelve words over and over until they envelope and define you results in a closer relationship with Jesus. Jesus becomes more clearly the Lord. The person who is praying discovers new-found peace.

Just as the transforming power of Jesus is encountered in the Eucharist, so prayer makes known to us the presence of the Risen Christ through the lives of others who enter our lives in Jesus' name.

We were sitting outside in the sun on a Tuesday afternoon when my cell phone rang. I struggled to pull it out and said, "Hello." An old, wavering voice said, "This is Ola. I called to tell you that S.J. died last Saturday."

S.J. was ninety-two years old, dead from advanced prostate cancer. He was born in Palestine, Texas, one of four children. His father was a lawyer; his grandfather a physician and one of the early graduates of Howard University after the end of the Civil War. After graduation from what is now Hampton University in Virginia, S.J. entered the University of Iowa to pursue a Ph.D. in clinical psychology.

Hampton Institute had been established soon after the Civil War by a Union general to provide education for freed slaves and for Native Americans. Mary Armstrong, the founder's much younger wife, was a vigorous woman who, like her husband, was years ahead of her time. She established and ran with an iron hand a family camp on Squam Lake, New Hampshire. All employees were Hampton students or graduate students who needed summer employment. S.J. spent several years working for Mrs. Armstrong, in charge of the outdoor operations of the camp, when he was an undergraduate at Hampton and then as a graduate student at Iowa.

Throughout every summer of my early years, from birth through college, my family spent each summer at this family camp on Squam Lake. For several of those summers, until World War II and S.J.'s service in the Navy, I was a curious, impressionable little boy, who found a mentor and teacher in S.J. Day after day, wherever he went, I went too. My memories of being a small shadow are strong. I followed him everywhere — watching, asking questions, riding in the back of his truck. No question was too trivial, explanations were thoughtful, detailed, memorable, often humorous. My mentor taught me important things:

- A young boy can find a true friend in an older man.

- Friendship spans decades, sustained by correspondence.

- Good teaching results from gentle affirmation, not challenge and demand.

- Accomplishment results from careful inquiry and hard work.

- Questions have answers.

- Differences between people are historical, social, economic, educational, and not racial.

- God in Christ is present with us.

The Christ we meet in the Eucharist, the Christ who stretched out his arms upon the cross and offered himself is the incarnate presence of God in our life. He comes again in those persons whom we encounter, whether announced or anonymous.

That presence is encouraged in the words of prayer.

 Lord Jesus Christ, Son of God, have mercy on me, a sinner.
Lord Jesus Christ, Son of God, have mercy on me, a sinner.
Lord Jesus Christ, Son of God, have mercy on me, a sinner.

Prayer is the practice of the presence of God. It happens in words. It happens in people.

 We give thanks to you, O God, for the goodness and love which you have made known to us in creation; in the calling of Israel to be your people; in your Word spoken through the prophets; and above all in the Word made flesh, Jesus, your Son. For in these last days you sent him to be incarnate from the Virgin Mary, to be the Savior

and Redeemer of the world. In him, you have delivered us from evil, and made us worthy to stand before you. In him, you have brought us out of error into truth, out of sin into righteousness, out of death into life.

(Eucharistic Prayer B, 368)

The power of this eucharistic prayer, whose roots are found in a very early liturgy of the Christian church, is the realization that through the course of time and history God is present. Thousands of years and several important, life-changing events are summarized. The sum total is that no matter who we are or where we are, God is with us. God is active and involved in the events of time and history and human interaction. If we are to see and hear and understand this, then we need to sharpen our eyes and ears and hearts to comprehend. God is always present, if we allow ourselves to be aware.

THEIR FRIENDSHIP BEGAN with a casual meeting. They became acquaintances, then professional colleagues, holding similar jobs in the same city. Common background and experience frequently brought them together. Then one of them lost his job, just as the other lost a key colleague. Was there a match? Could they work together? They decided to give it a try. It might even work.

It worked more than well; their professional relationship became deeper, their friendship richer. The interlocking web that bound them together was strong, at its heart the conviction that goodness and love were evident in the trust, confidence, and belief they held in each other. Time together was marked by honesty. Friendship was no accident.

The circumstances that brought them together continued to unfold as if foreordained. Although this could not have been true, the ways friendship unfolded and deepened continued to suggest it. If one is able to make it clear to another the power of the present moment, that moment will contain the promise of new revelation.

When crippling, sometimes life-threatening illness struck one and then the other, they found they were brought together in prayer. Prayer led to new understanding. As one crisis abated and there was room for hope, one wrote:

Just before Christmas as I was being shuffled in and out of operating rooms, MRIs, CT scans, and things were looking from bad to worse. I had time to think and pray about the indecision and unknowns that were facing us. Suddenly there were two words I focused on: *path* and *journey*. If I truly believed in God, then I must believe in the path, the Way that God has given me to follow. I need not fear it, God has watched over me and has already made the decision. The journey has been rich and wonderful, and if it is to stop now...so be it. I suddenly stopped worrying completely. I never gave the cancer concerns another thought. I just knew that I was on the journey that had been set aside for me...come what may.

The opportunity to be brought out of error into truth, out of sin into righteousness, out of death into life is the hope, the possibility that makes daily life possible. Without it, all that we do is worth nothing, just one damn thing after another. So it is that we ground ourselves in this hope, constantly present and renewed, made clear in the Eucharist and available to each of us through our life of daily prayer.

✠ God of all power, Ruler of the Universe, you are worthy of glory and praise. At your command all things came to be: the vast expanse of interstellar space, galaxies, suns, the planets in their courses, and this fragile earth, our island home. From the primal elements you brought forth the human race, and blessed us with memory, reason, and skill. You made us the rulers of creation. But we turned against you, and betrayed your trust; and we turned against one another. (Eucharistic Prayer C, 370)

This eucharistic prayer catches the hearer and participant up in its poetry and poignant description of the world we have been given. We have been given everything, yet we have been irresponsible in so many ways. Too many of these ways are irretrievable and unredeemable.

The words are reminiscent of the ten petitions in the Litany of Penitence appointed for use on Ash Wednesday that call us to self-examination through prayer and contemplation.

✠ We have not loved you with our whole heart, and mind, and strength. We have not loved our neighbors as ourselves. We have not forgiven others, as we have been forgiven.

We have been deaf to your call to serve, as Christ served us. We have not been true to the mind of Christ. We have grieved your Holy Spirit.

We confess to you, Lord, all our past unfaithfulness: the pride, hypocrisy, and impatience of our lives,

Our self-indulgent appetites and ways and our exploitation of other people,

Our anger at our own frustration, and our envy of those more fortunate than ourselves,

Our intemperate love of worldly goods and comforts, and our dishonesty in daily life and work,

Our negligence in prayer and worship, and our failure to commend the faith that is in us,

Accept our repentance, Lord, for the wrongs we have done: for our blindness to human need and suffering, and our indifference to injustice and cruelty.

For all false judgments, for uncharitable thoughts toward our neighbors, and for our prejudice and contempt towards those who differ from us,

For our waste and pollution of your creation, and our lack of concern for those who come after us.   (BCP, 267–68)

The power of the phrase so often quoted from Eucharistic Prayer C, *this fragile earth, our island home,* brings us up short. The grace, good fortune and abundance given to each of us, who is a resident on this earth created by God, is finite. We are finite. The planet on which we live is finite. The gifts we have been given, which should be well used, not wasted and abused, offer abundance, but if we are mindless, thoughtless and wasteful, we hasten our own demise and destruction.

Here at the beginning of this prayer of consecration, we are reminded of our need for reflection and self-examination. The time to pause and take stock is always available in prayer, the practice of the presence of God. This gift is given to be used in all times and places by all sorts and conditions of the people of this earth.

When the hour had come for him to be glorified by you, his heavenly Father, having loved his own who were in the world, he loved them to the end; at supper with them he took bread, and when he had given thanks to you, he broke it, and gave it to his disciples, and said, "Take, eat: This is my Body which is given for you. Do this for the remembrance of me."

After supper he took the cup of wine; and when he had given thanks, he gave it to them, and said, "Drink this, all of you. This is my Blood of the new Covenant,

which is shed for you and for many for the forgiveness of sins. Whenever you drink it, do this for the remembrance of me." (Eucharistic Prayer D, 374)

Remembrance is key to the event of the Eucharist and its effect in our lives, both at the moment when it happens and throughout the days that follow.

Remembrance means that what happened once in the past is brought into this present when we experience it again, as if for the very first time. In these words of institution, we are present with Jesus in that upper room on the night before he died for us on the cross, on what we remember as Good Friday. What happened once and for all time then happens again in our midst right now.

The selectiveness of memory is a mystery. Most events, once they have happened, drift off into the oblong blur we call the past and are seldom revisited. We are told that everything that has ever happened to us remains buried in the mass of tissue and nerve-endings known as the brain. Admiral James Stockdale, imprisoned for nine years during the Vietnam War, reported that in the silence of his prison cell he was able to remember virtually all of the passages of the Bible he had learned as a child in a Methodist Sunday school in Indiana. So too for us. What happened once remains with us, only we do not necessarily remember, until the special moment when we call that event forth into the present and experience it again.

There are events, however, the central moments of a lifetime, that remain ready to enter the present whenever we summon them, which we do, again and again. They are special, singular, life-changing. The more we think of them, the more others will come to mind.

- Seeing each other for the first time
- Falling in love
- Being all alone and not knowing what to do
- The wedding
- Seeing your child for the very first time
- Ordination
- Conversations that changed everything

AS HE REACHED OUT to put his hand on the doorknob, he noticed that his fingers trembled. He couldn't be that nervous, but apparently he was. He pushed the door open and walked into the room. At the far end, an expanse of glass gave a full, sunlit view of the harbor, late on this holiday morning. Four gentlemen dressed in tweed jackets and bow ties turned, almost as one, to greet him. Each was holding a glass of sherry. There were hand shakes, followed by pleasantries, the kind of conversation about the weather and game scores that he'd learned to handle while repeating, over and over again, the names that went with the faces he'd just met for the first time. He felt himself settle into a calm that surrounded this routine that he knew well.

In what seemed like no time at all, a young woman in black dress and white apron appeared from the room beyond to say that lunch was on the table. They entered a small, corporate dining room. He was seated with his back to the window that also looked onto the harbor. The first real question of the interview hung in the air, still unspoken. He could almost smell it, the real beginning of this conversation. Would it be the same wrong kind of question he'd heard often in the past?

The wrong question would go something like this. "Sir, if you were headmaster of our school, if you were in charge, please tell us what you would do? Would you outline your plan of operations for the first five years?"

How was he, or anyone, supposed to answer such a question? If he did so, he was an idiot. How could he possibly answer such a question, when he knew nothing, absolutely nothing, about this particular school or how to run it? How could he? He'd never even seen the school, let alone worked in it. But if he failed to answer such a question, when asked, he would appear to be a fool, for after all, he'd agreed to the interview.

He could feel that initial question forming on the lips of the man to his right, who turned and said, "You're good to take the time to come and speak with us. You have such good school experience that we hope it's safe to assume you've given some thought to what it might be like for you if you ever ran a school. When you have such thoughts, what comes first to mind? What would you most want to do? We'd be interested to know."

He couldn't breathe a sigh of relief, not yet, that would be embarrassing, but he felt the need. This was a different kind of question, one that opened doors, allowed for honesty and imagination. These men meant to engage a fellow human being, not a thing, whom they'd hire the way they'd buy a car.

Then he did take a deep breath, opened his mouth and said the first thing that came to mind: "Teach. The first thing I'd want to do is teach. I love to teach."

Had he said the wrong thing? He must have. These men were looking for someone to run a school, and he'd just told them the first thing he wanted to do was teach. No doubt they'd clear their throats and tell him to get back in his car and spend the rest of his life teaching.

That was not what they did. The conversation continued at an ever-increasing level of intensity. Two hours later when he did get up and drive back home, he knew that they would offer him the job.

Some time later he learned that his first answer had been exactly what they wanted to hear. They were looking for a headmaster who would be involved in the life of the school and spend time with students, especially in the classroom. This made all the difference. This was a school where he could be himself and find fulfillment. The memory of the single question and his answer motivated everything he did.

Events, words, moments that change the course of a lifetime and influence everything that comes after them live in memory. Such memory molds the present. Such memory *becomes* the present. Such memory brings alive the moment that changed our lives in the past. Life-changing events — beginning with Jesus at the Last Supper — come forth and are relived, for they have changed everything.

✠ "Take, eat: This is my Body, which is given for you. Do this for the remembrance of me...." "Drink this, all of you: This is my Blood of the new Covenant, which is shed for you and for many for the forgiveness of sins. Whenever you drink it, do this for the remembrance of me."

These words paint a picture from the past and in so doing, bring that event into the present. Once present, it happens all over again for us and to us. When it happens, Jesus Christ is in our midst. Not just for an instant but for the abiding present. He comes to us and dwells with us. When he does, we are at prayer.

✠ Eternal God, heavenly Father,
you have graciously accepted us as living members
of your Son our Savior Jesus Christ,
and you have fed us with spiritual food
in the Sacrament of his Body and Blood.
Send us now into the world in peace,
and grant us strength and courage
to love and serve you
with gladness and singleness of heart;
through Christ our Lord. Amen.

(The Post-Communion Prayer, 365)

We are now *living members* whom God sends *into the world in peace*. The Eucharist does not end with the final "Amen." The Eucharist continues as we go forth.

Christ has no hands, no feet, no eyes, ears, mouths, or minds save those that we take into the world in his name. This means that we are never alone. It also means that as we go, wherever we go, Christ goes with us.

Chapter Nine

PEACE AT THE LAST

Almighty God, our heavenly Father, who settest the solitary in families: We commend to thy continual care the homes in which thy people dwell. Put far from them, we beseech thee, every root of bitterness, the desire of vainglory, and the pride of life. Fill them with faith, virtue, knowledge, temperance, patience, godliness. Knit together in constant affection those who, in holy wedlock, have been made one flesh. Turn the hearts of the parents to the children, and the hearts of the children to the parents; and so enkindle fervent charity among us all, that we may evermore be kindly affectioned one to another; through Jesus Christ our Lord. Amen.   (For Families, 828–29)

One of the final prayers in the marriage service contains the words, "that their home may be a haven of blessing and of peace." Home is a quality of life, an atmosphere that exists between two people who have been made one flesh in marriage. A family originates with these two persons,

140

and this family, with or without children, establishes the ambiance called home.

"A house is not a home," but within that house a home may be created. The concept of "home" has been pre-empted by real estate brokers to convince the customer to purchase a dwelling in order to acquire a home. This is folly. A house is not a home. A house is a house, and only a house, although what we call "home" may come to exist within that house. A home is not defined by physical space but by the family who creates it. Family begins in marriage, when two become one, and grows to embrace all those who join this family and choose to be defined by home.

A child senses instinctively whether a space is a home or not, just as you did when you first entered someone else's house. You felt it; you could even smell it. A home was a place you wanted to be; it drew you. and you went there as often as you could. You also knew spaces that were not havens of blessing and peace, and you stayed away from them.

Home is a place that invites you, a place where blessing and peace abide and abound. In this prayer "For Families" we commend to God the homes in which God's people dwell, knowing that family is God's creation, made possible for God's people to live together in community and in peace.

The idea and reality of the family living together in the atmosphere that is a home is a profoundly religious concept, deeply rooted in the Judeo-Christian tradition. This prayer, carefully crafted in the late 1800s by Bishop Frederick Dan Huntington, drew heavily on biblical sources: Psalm 68, the Letter to the Hebrews, Galatians, Genesis, and Malachi. The ideas it expresses are centered in the heart of our faith and tradition.

These ideas pertain to our traditional understandings of family and family units, but they apply equally well — sometimes even more so — to other groups. Parishes and schools are such groups. These are gatherings of people committed to ongoing care for and with one another.

These were my thoughts as I undertook to transform a formerly all-boys' school for coeducation. This required a new mission statement. Since this was an old neighborhood school built around a small group of families, the idea of family molded the future. The mission statement reads:

> Growth, knowledge, the discovery of value and personal worth all come from the family: not only the family into which we were born, the family into which we may marry, but other families as well. This school hopes to be such a family in which each member cares and to which each member contributes, a family of interaction and respect, personal integrity and commitment to excellence, a family where one may develop the mind, the body, and the spirit for a life of service.

We live surrounded by family. This experience, common to every human being, is mythic, embodying what is central in human experience. Family is a symbol pointing beyond itself. Even if you grew up in a foster home and knew no biological parents, you belong to a family that is greater than anything you know firsthand. The secular reality is "the family of man." The theological reality is the body of Christ.

This is why family — reality, myth, symbol — is powerful, why it shapes and changes lives. We hope and pray to belong to a family in which each member cares and to which each member contributes, a family of interaction and respect, personal integrity and commitment to excellence, a family where one may develop the mind, the body and the spirit for a life of service.

The reality that is family evolves through prayer. This is why we hope and pray that we live in homes that enkindle fervent charity among us all, that we may evermore be kindly affectioned (as The Book of Common Prayer states it) one to another, through Jesus Christ our Lord.

Family is not easy to understand or to model. It is uncomfortable to belong to a family. What makes family possible is to believe that it exists, to pray for its establishment and its support, to understand and state that it is an actuality. The popular song "We are Family" makes sense. Say it, affirm it, believe it. It will happen. But only if we invest ourselves in the creation of family. Only if we pray for, with and in families, remembering that the most common statement about prayer is, "Do you believe prayers are answered?"

The answer: "Well, yes and no, but first tell me about your prayers and your life of prayer. For what do you pray and why?"

Family is created because we intend it. We mean it to happen. At the heart of this intention it is necessary that self-consciously and deliberately we say — in words and actions — that we mean to be a family, We pray our family into being. It is not automatic.

Family is deeply rooted in our tradition, handed down to us through our faith. Family is integral, essential to everything it means to be a Christian. Family happens when we pray about it and for it.

TWO FATHERS MET in Manhattan at their daughters' Jewish nursery school and discovered that their own fathers had both come from the same village in Ukraine. They then discovered that both fathers had been loaded onto the same boxcar leading to the same concentration camp on the same day. Then they discovered that one of their fathers had escaped by ripping out a board over a window and jumping out. He joined up with some partisans, and somehow survived the war. Then they discovered that before he jumped, he had lifted up a younger, shorter boy and pushed him out of the boxcar before him. That boy also wandered the forests of Ukraine and also came to America after the war. Both fathers had recently died in New York and had no idea that their sons were sending their granddaughters to the same nursery school. They did not know that the little girls would have a play date in Manhattan because of what happened in a boxcar in Ukraine some sixty-three years ago. That little hole in that boxcar was big enough to have room for a play date and a future.

O God, by whom the meek are guided in judgment, and light rises up in darkness for the godly: Grant us, in all our doubts and uncertainties, the grace to ask what you would have us to do, that the Spirit of wisdom may save us from all false choices, and that in your light we may see light, and in your straight path may not stumble; through Jesus Christ our Lord. Amen. (For Guidance, 832)

Meek does not mean what we think it means. The Bible describes Moses as meek. He was far from timid; his impetuosity, temper, rage, and determination resulted in God barring him from the Promised Land. Moses was no milk toast.

Moses was meek because he understood who he was in the eyes of God. Meek is a synonym for *humble,* a word whose roots are found in the word *humus* that means earth. To be humble, to be meek, is to know who you really are in the eyes of God. God sees you as you are, not as the person you hope to be or the person you imagine yourself to be, but the person you are.

Those who know and see themselves as they are, these are the people who are able to open their lives to God and be guided by God's judgment.

O God, by whom the meek are guided in judgment. If we know who we are, really are, then we may be guided by

God's presence in prayer. The meek are people for whom *light rises up in darkness.*

The difference between light and dark is no mystery. We awake to it each morning, suddenly conscious, but afraid. It happens to me every morning, encased in the dark, I am afraid. Afraid of what? Like Harry and Edna in Edward Albee's "A Delicate Balance," I am afraid of *nothing.* I am afraid of the nothing that is the dark. There is nothing there, but I am afraid. But the light that rises up in the darkness changes all that. God is in the dark, but, at least for me, God is not fully present until God's light has again entered my life.

The darkness surrounds me with doubts and uncertainties, but then the grace to ask what I should do comes in the light — what I should think, how I should begin this day. Out of bed, I follow my feet that lead me to begin the activity of the day; first to accomplish something I postponed the previous evening. It happens in God's light. In that light the Spirit of wisdom, God's spirit, may save me from false choices that are always at hand. In God's light we shall see light to find the straight path and not to stumble.

One of the new insights that comes with advancing age is that to fall is to fail, perhaps finally. The one thing one must not do is to stumble. If one stumbles and falls, the result could be permanently crippling. Fear of falling takes on a whole new meaning. Suddenly you want to hold on, hold on for dear life, for if you fall, fall away from whom you are in God's light, then you may very well cease to be.

Any remote chance that you ever felt to be self-reliant and all-powerful vanishes. God's presence is not a vain hope, but the single reality that makes daily life possible. It all begins in the light, the need for light, God's light, and the reality is that without it you may stumble and fall from grace, away from God and be no more.

The words of this Collect for Guidance, added to The Book of Common Prayer in 1928 from William Bright's *Ancient Collects*, describe the condition of prayer that marks the opening of each day and guide us into the light that is God, step by step, saving us from false choices and making it possible not to stumble.

THE FEAR THAT GRIPPED HIM in the early morning dark was well-founded. None of it was fantasy. When he finally realized that dawn was approaching and made himself get out of bed, exercise, bathe, and dress, the first thing he'd have to do was to get on the phone and ask the lawyers. There would be two of them in the conference call. First the one and then the other would tell him what to do each step of the way to get through another day, just one more day.

It was no way to live, and he hated it. If he knew one thing, one thing that might save him from false choices, it was that he needed to make a change. This was no way to live — day after day after day. No way to live. He was getting out of this mess and finding a new way, a wholly different way, to begin each day.

But today, right now, he had no choice, but to move forward and get the job done. He would undertake what he knew he needed to do, as best he was able, all the time keeping his life, his mind, his eyes and ears open to the Presence that would uplift and support him.

He may only be one small person, but he was not alone, never alone.

O God of peace, who has taught us that in returning and rest we shall be saved, in quietness and in confidence shall be our strength: By the might of your Spirit lift us, we pray you, to your presence, where we may be still and know that you are God; through Jesus Christ our Lord. Amen. (For Quiet Confidence, 832)

Silence is God's first language and all other languages are poor translations.

HIS SMALL, PORTABLE TAPE RECORDER refused to play. The time had come for the morning walk. There was only one thing to do — walk in silence.

The first indications of sunrise were beginning to appear. The bluebirds and red-winged black birds were awake, every one of them silent. Small flocks of geese — five here and eight there — flew black and honking across the sky, talking back and forth to one another as they went. Did they have really important matters to discuss at this hour? Or did they talk to keep themselves company? More than fifty of them now rose from beyond the trees on the distant shore and crossed the scattered pink and gray clouds, heading north. The sight resembled a Benson etching. Far, far down the straight, deserted country road a herd of deer crossed, soundlessly, from one side to the other, then slouched down and under the rail fence spanning a little gully.

Much to see, only an occasional sound. The silence was not perfect, but what silence there was spoke.

Pulling the earmuffs from my pocket, I clamped them over my head to insulate my ears and walked on, only aware of the muffled *thump, thump* of my feet hitting the pavement. Otherwise... nothing. This was the way to begin the day. Prayer is first silence. God speaks in the silence.

St. John of the Cross wrote, "The Father spoke one word from all eternity, and he spoke it in silence, and it is in silence that we hear it."

Soon after John Coburn retired as Bishop of Massachusetts, he served for one semester as a visiting professor of spirituality at Virginia Theological Seminary. His course on prayer for entering students had to be expanded from one to three sections to accommodate those who wanted to join — the entire class. Bishop Coburn opened each class with this prayer "for quiet confidence," and ten minutes of silence followed before he spoke again.

Coburn reported that as the years passed, he received several letters saying that the most valuable part of the course was the silence. "My job was to do nothing," he would say and then laugh. His role was to introduce the voice of God.

Lord, make us instruments of your peace. Where there is hatred, let us sow love; where there is injury, pardon; where there is discord, union; where there is doubt, faith; where there is despair, hope; where there is darkness, light; where there is sadness, joy. Grant that we may not so much seek to be consoled as to console; to be understood as to understand; to be loved as to love. For it is in giving that we receive; it is in pardoning that we are pardoned; and it is in dying that we are born to eternal life. Amen. (A Prayer attributed to St. Francis, 833)

This prayer, whose true source is lost but is attributed to St. Francis, sets a tone none can escape. The words envelop us with challenge and hope. Their intention is to describe the natural but very demanding effort to make a contribution. The choice is always ours, and when we use this prayer, we are encouraged to make the effort to create a better world. It all begins with me.

The goal set before us is peace. The word means wholeness. It means the intention to be at one with one another and with ourselves and with God. This is what will make a difference. Peace: it is elusive, difficult and complex, yet it is very simple.

The Prayer of St. Francis gives the promise to help make us instruments of God's peace, states the choices offered, day by day, through the endless opportunities given to each of us. Reflect on where and how each choice might be part of our life today. Do it right now.

Where there is hatred, let us sow love. Her face was red, contorted. She was shaking, uncontrollably, seemed unable to put together a cohesive sentence. "You! You! You!" she stammered. I had no idea what to say. I reached out and hugged her. Neither of us spoke. The shaking stopped.

Where there is injury, pardon. What I'd done had been wrong, really wrong, and I knew it. There was only one thing to say. "I'm sorry," I said. "I can't tell you how sorry. Please forgive me."

There was no response. I froze. Only silence and then there was more silence. Finally, again, I said, "I'm sorry. I can't tell you how sorry. Please forgive me."

And then heard, "Of course I forgive you."

Where there is discord, union. It wasn't my fight, and I wanted no part of it. Let the two of them sort it out for themselves. But they weren't going to do that. Not today or tomorrow or any day. The whole thing would just grow and grow. Pretty soon the mess would involve us all. Every single person around this table would take sides. Then it would be too late.

I cleared my throat to announce I had something to say, and before I knew it, I was saying it. "No one is going to come out of this a winner. No one. Could you just agree that you disagree? Let's move forward."

151

Where there is doubt, faith. " . . . I just don't know. I just don't know. I don't know what I believe."

She was repeating herself, senselessly, almost unknowingly. I thought to myself, "I do know. I know what I believe. It may not be of any help to her to hear that, but it's worth a try." And so I said it. I told her what I believed and why.

What I said was that in a time like this, you don't continue to weigh all the options. You stop saying, "Well on the one hand . . . and then on the other." No, that's not what you need right now. What you need to say is this: "I've weighed all the options, and I'm going with this one." And then you move ahead, into the future. That's the way it has to be.

Where there is despair, hope. The devastation was so complete, so massive after the hurricane that after a while I couldn't turn on the television or even open a newspaper. Everything about it was hopeless, completely hopeless.

After a while she just couldn't stand it anymore. One conversation led to another and another. Then a plan to involve first people from here and then from there. Then the decision what to do.

On the following Monday she was on a plane with six volunteers heading for the disaster zone. After arriving, they camped out for a week in a school and spent their days clearing seven house lots to be ready for temporary housing.

Where there is darkness, light. Tears, too often, marked the night, the dark. But joy comes in the morning. He knew this, and he believed it. He rolled over, closed his eyes and prayed, over and over again, "Dear God. I give myself to thee this night, thine only, thine ever to be." The next thing he knew, light was coming in through the window.

Where there is sadness, joy. The day was sunny, one of the first real days of spring. The infant boy had lived but a few minutes, long enough to be baptized by a caring pediatrician present for the emergency delivery to care for the child. While the baby's mother stayed in the hospital, his father and his grandparents drove together the forty miles to the colonial graveyard where the boy would be buried. He asked me to come along and we rode in the front seat together with his parents in the back, silent.

Everyone was silent. There was not much to say, casual conversation awkward and inappropriate. But something told my friend that the only kind of communication that made any sense was laughter and he quoted a line from last night's late-night talk show. I laughed. He joined me, and we laughed together — hard. The parents in the back seat joined in. The relaxation was palpable. Pain still filled the car, but laughter diluted it, helped to make it more bearable. I was not sure how he did it. The laughter continued. There'd be time for tears at the graveside.

Grant that we may not so much seek to be consoled as to console. "It's not always about you, you know," she said. "It's not always about you. Sometimes, just occasionally, you might think about someone else. There are thirteen other people in this family, and some of them, all

153

of them, need your love and concern and interest. Think about that. Just think about that."

To be understood, as to understand. The pain was unbearable. She had been shut out, forgotten, cast aside. Being fired was one thing, but the way it had been handled had made it ten times worse than it might have been. All she wanted to do was to crawl into a corner, cry and feel sorry for herself.

But tonight they were all going to gather around one table to talk, to come clean, to hold hands and move forward as one family, persons whose lives were all involved. Everyone of them had lost just as much as she'd lost. If she thought about them, concentrated on what was important for each of the others, it would make a big difference for the family. She promised herself to try.

To be loved, as to love. He knew that they all loved him. They said so, and it was clear. But he'd never, not really, let himself go, allowed himself to think and then to say, to tell each one of them, how much he thought of each and every one of them every day. Their days together were numbered, and he resolved to count each one of those days as if it were his last and to let them hear from him that they mattered to him, to tell them how much he loved them, really loved them.

He did it. Love grew.

For it is in giving that we receive. He was nervous about the appointment. As he sat down with this prominent man he had no idea of where and how to start. Then he remembered that his youngest child, a son, was in difficulty.

There'd even been a story in the newspaper. Probably no one dared mention it to him, ask how he felt and how he dealt with it.

Across the big oak desk that must have been ten feet wide, the younger man asked, "Tell me about Sam. How's it going?"

Those were the last words he spoke for ten minutes. There was much to tell and hear about Sam. As the father spoke, he relaxed, loosened, opened up. The rest of the conversation was easy.

As he left the office, he thought to himself, "If we spent more time caring about others, expressing love and concern, life would be smoother, easier, more natural."

It is in pardoning that we are pardoned. He was an old friend. They had known each other for more than thirty years. His only sister had just been killed in a senseless accident, and he was still raw, missing her every day and hour. Theirs was a very close family of five siblings, and after each had married and had children, they still found the time and the way to gather regularly.

He was talking about how much he missed her. "She was good, really good, at saying 'Thank you.' She meant it. But she could never say 'That's all right.' Or, 'Forget it.' When you say that, healing takes place. The circle is closed. Life goes on. But you have to offer forgiveness if you are both to be forgiven and remain brother and sister.

"And so I told her. I said, 'Martha, come right out and say, "That's all right." It will change everything.' She did. And it did."

And it is in dying that we are born to eternal life. The time had come to say good-bye and leave. It had been a good run. Ten years. She'd loved doing the job, every bit of it. Now it was over, time to move on to something new and different in another place. Transition would not be easy. She knew that. She'd been here before. Everything that begins ends. Now it was time to move forward, toward the new life that waited.

✠ O Lord, support us all the day long, until the shadows lengthen, and the evening comes, and the busy world is hushed, and the fever of life is over, and our work is done. Then in thy mercy, grant us a safe lodging, and a holy rest, and peace at the last. Amen.

(Prayer for Evening, 833)

Composed of phrases from a sermon by John Henry Newman, this prayer is a statement of completion. We pray for the completion of a day, for the completion of our work, for the completion of our life. There is nothing sad about the prayer. It is restful, peaceful, concerned with fulfillment, as we anticipate something more: the eternal.

This is a prayer for the end of the day, but it is also a prayer for all seasons. There is no time that we do not look forward to a safe lodging, a holy rest, and peace at the last. These are descriptive words, poetry to describe the dimension for which we hope: the eternal.

The past is gone, not forgotten, present in memory, but gone. The future is unknown, unpredictable, awaiting discovery. All we know for sure, right now, is the present, this moment. Into this moment God comes. In this moment God dwells. It is this moment that God transforms. It is this moment, this eternal, that we describe as *safe lodging, holy rest, and peace at the last.*

SHE'D WAITED ALL DAY, all week — or was it a lifetime — for this to happen.

The children had scattered years ago. No regrets, joy in fact, but she missed them. How she missed them. Every day, several times every day.

It had to be — each one living her own life. But there were times when she longed for the slam of the kitchen door late in the afternoon, noisy suppers around the blue table, screams from the upstairs hall, when everyone needed to finish homework and go to bed.

None of that was any longer part of her life. Tantrums were so far in the past that she missed them. Each child grown, middle-aged, was surrounded by the cries of her own children. They could no longer be all together. It would be wrong. Still she wished, longed, for just a few moments, when they could all gather in peace and be at rest in the arms of one another, in the arms of the everlasting.

Now it was about to happen. It would be merely an instant in the great economy of time. The anticipation had been intense, fulfilling, reminding her of the old Pan American advertisement she saw once on a highway billboard, "Getting there is half the fun." For her, getting this far had been more than a succession of days and years, it had been all of the fun. Completion was close, and achievement and fulfillment. Pain and loss and sorrow were inevitable but masked by memories of reunion.

It was about to happen. Every member of the family would be coming through the kitchen door. It might be the last time or another in a whole succession of times. It didn't matter. When they were all together, time stood still. Memory was now. Future was now. This was it. She didn't have to remind herself.

For some people there is one place where everything that ever happened — or so it seems — is gathered together. It is the place where life began and continued. Not literally, but it is the place that keeps popping up in your head and won't leave you alone. It might have been a favorite chair in your grandparents' house or a particular corner in the neighborhood drugstore. For some it was one weekend each year when you went off, just you, with your parents to the same special place and talked and told stories and read books and ate special meals.

Maybe it was a lake, a mountain cabin, a place at the beach — or none of those, nothing that remote or unusual. The place may have been part of your life for only an instant, or again and again through the years, or for the years of childhood, and then it was no more. But for everyone there is that place, a place of hope and peace and rest. And the fact that it was once, once upon a time, means that it will continue to be again — and again.

It is this place for which we pray. It is this place to which we return when we pray at anytime, but especially when we use the words of this evening prayer.

When in the early morning dark, I say the words of this prayer, they call forth the hymn by John Greenleaf Whittier. Whittier wrote his hymn during summers he spent at his cabin on Squam Lake, New Hampshire. This is the place to which I return in my mind when I pray.

O Sabbath rest by Galilee! O calm of hills above,
Where Jesus knelt to share with thee the silence of
    eternity
Interpreted by love!
Drop they still dews of quietness, till all our strivings
    cease;
Take from our souls the strain and stress, and let our
    ordered lives confess
The beauty of thy peace.

Breathe through the heats of our desire thy coolness
    and thy balm;
Let sense be dumb, let flesh retire; speak through the
    earthquake, wind, and fire,
O still small voice of calm.

Whittier uses biblical images, word pictures. He recalls Jesus on the Sea of Galilee and Elijah on Mount Horeb.

His words bring forth my own childhood and gather together what is reality for me right now. Through word and memory, the present opens into an understanding of the presence of God through history and the life, death and resurrection of Jesus Christ. This is gathered into the present — the eternal — that is right now.

All of this happens in prayer made real through words, thoughts, intentions from the past, words that bring the presence of God into this present, which is eternal.

Chapter Ten

THANKS IN ALL THINGS

Accept, O Lord, our thanks and praise for all that you have done for us. We thank you for the splendor of the whole creation, for the beauty of this world, for the wonder of life, and for the mystery of love.

We thank you for the blessing of family and friends, and for the loving care which surrounds us on every side.

We thank you for setting us at tasks which demand our best efforts, and for leading us to accomplishments which satisfy and delight us.

We thank you also for those disappointments and failures that lead us to acknowledge our dependence on you alone.

Above all, we thank you for your Son Jesus Christ; for the truth of his Word and the example of his life; for his steadfast obedience, by which he overcame temptation; for his dying, through which he overcame death; and for his rising to life again, in which we are raised to the life of your kingdom.

Grant us the gift of your Spirit, that we may know Christ and make him known; and through him, at all times and in all places, may give thanks to you in all things. Amen.

(A General Thanksgiving, 836)

These words were written in 1965 for Memorial Church at Harvard by the Preacher to the University, Charles Philip Price. They offer a complete theology and a firm foundation for private prayer. These words also embody the energy of the author: a teacher, preacher, pastor, friend, mentor, and guide. He molded and changed countless persons, influenced how and why they learn, what they learned, what they believe. His teaching, writing and living personified the height and depth, the joy and pain, of everything he knew and believed. Standing directly in front of his theology class, deadly serious, he shook his finger and said, "Remember Tertullian. Remember Tertullian. Once upon a time, a very long time ago, Tertullian had a bright idea. It's called the Trinity. Remember that. You remember that. You too might have a bright idea."

The General Thanksgiving gives us the framework for our life of prayer. It begins with *accept* — the best and only thing we can do, each day of our lives. All we are given is a gift; therefore, even during moments of the greatest crisis — illness, death, loss — we accept. Whatever may be happening, it is happening to me, right now. What's to be done? Move into it and move through it and beyond it. It is not all there will ever be. This too shall pass. Other times, many times, different times, new times, await you.

162

Even times when skies will be bright, winds fair, the world full of hope and promise; therefore . . .

Accept, O Lord, our thanks and praise for all that you have done for us. When my childhood friend called, just before my heart surgery, to say, "It's better than the alternative," he meant, "It's better to *be*. It's better to be alive. Whatever it is that is happening right now is far, far better than never to have been."

We awake each day to new possibility. We awake to live in the presence of God, full of thanks and praise. Life is a gift. None of it is earned. Accept it, with thanks and praise.

We thank you for the splendor of the whole creation. The prayer places us in an expansive, overwhelming framework — the splendor of the whole creation.

Growing up during World War II created an ever-present, all-inclusive framework. Air raid drills and blackouts on the northeastern seaboard were real and scary. The world was in grave conflict; danger was everywhere. Mother constantly spoke of how fortunate we were to be born and live in the United States. It was a gift. We were all intensely patriotic, but the awareness of the reality that we had been given so much went far beyond patriotism. We were steeped in the profound realization that we do not choose to be nor where we are born. Heritage is not a choice. Heritage is a gift that creates the framework for all of life. Individual lives are minuscule, but, fortunately, we are surrounded by the splendor of the whole creation.

Splendor is but the beginning. There is more. The full glory of splendor is received, thanks to the beauty of this world, the wonder of life, and the mystery of love. Every single bit of what is meant by beauty, wonder and mystery we take for granted. Why? When encountered in their fullness, they are beyond our wildest imagining. Each enhances the other. Each one, startling as it is, finds luster, tone and brilliance in the other, but the three are fitly framed together by the mystery of love.

Were it not for the mystery of love, the colors would not be so bright, the breeze so soft, the promise of the day so compelling. Splendor, beauty and wonder become clearer, brighter and lovelier, thanks to the mystery of love.

We thank you for the blessing of family and friends, and for the loving care which surrounds us on every side. We begin each day, thankful that we have been given life and knowing that family and friends surround us on every side. We are not alone; we are never alone. This is something we so easily, too easily, forget: we are surrounded by those who care and support, if we have eyes to see, ears to hear and hearts to understand.

This is the principle reason it is possible to thank God for *setting us at tasks which demand our best efforts, and for leading us to accomplishments which satisfy and delight us.* The support of friends and family makes possible the pursuit of tasks that demand effort and satisfy and delight.

But not always. Nobody's perfect. Everyone makes mistakes, mistakes that remind us that we are human;

therefore, we thank God *also for those disappointments and failures that lead us to acknowledge our dependence on you alone.* It is a very uncomfortable experience to know that we are without the strength of purpose and accomplishment in which we take so much pride, but it's fact. We learn more from our failures than from our successes.

THE ENTIRE FAMILY had gathered around the table, expanded to its absolute largest size, for Thanksgiving. Dinner served, grace said, the ensuing silence was broken by an announcement:. "I'd like to know the one thing that everyone at this table is most thankful for." She stopped to take a breath, and then added, "Who wants to begin?"

For a short while, no one spoke and then a little girl's voice offered, "Mommy and Daddy." From the other side of the table, "Amen to that," commented her father.

After a brief silence, the rest of the family caught on and joined in, one after the other. Statements of thanks varied, some more thoughtful than others, but the thoughts continued to flow until only one person remained.

The oldest member of the family was sitting next to her granddaughter, who had started the whole process with the words, "Mommy and Daddy." Slowly, one after another, everyone realized that she was getting ready to speak. For what could she possibly be thankful? The past year had been one long nightmare. Fifteen years ago she'd made a bad marriage to her second husband, who was sitting across from her now, looking at the ceiling and rolling his eyes, perpetually bored. He'd lost his job ten years ago, had refused to find work, spent each day all day, drinking. Meanwhile his wife worked six and sometimes seven days a week to support the family.

The table waited, and then waited some more, before she spoke. "I'm thankful," she said, "more thankful than I can ever say for my Lord and Savior, Jesus Christ."

The moment called for response, something should be said, but no one spoke.

We thank you also for those disappointments and failures that lead us to acknowledge our dependence on you alone.

EVERYONE REMEMBERED that she had once been a beautiful woman. Not that her photograph would ever have appeared in a fashion magazine, but she was a radiant person, usually smiling, a woman full of love and hope, a joyful companion, until her operation changed all that.

The cancer began in her right ear; the first symptom was persistent earache. The pain gradually abated, then returned, more frequent and severe. The initial diagnosis was not hopeful. Surgery was immediate, the operation a success. She was pronounced cured, but the surgeon had removed half of her face and turned her into a scarred, wizened, angry woman, who bore little resemblance, physically or any other way, to the person she once had been. Her husband left her. She lost all her bearings and began to drink heavily.

The road to recovery was neither quick nor easy, but she took it. Alcoholics Anonymous was invaluable. So too the rediscovery in a whole new way of the faith that had surrounded her in her early life well through college and into her adult life.

Her local parish and especially a small and devoted prayer group surrounded and enveloped her in the love of Christ. She was transformed. Wherever she went and with whomever she spoke it became clear that she embodied the power and presence of the Holy Spirit. Her energies, professional and personal, became devoted to helping other people with facial disfigurement to face the world and lead productive lives. As she had been changed, so she became an agent for change because of, not just in spite of, the profound disappointment that had marked and marred her life.

Disappointments and failures are a constant reminder that we are not alone. We live not for ourselves only, but we live and move and have our being through Christ who strengthens us. It is for this reason that we pray: *Above all, we thank you for your Son Jesus Christ; for the truth of his Word and the example of his life; for his steadfast obedience, by which he overcame temptation; for his dying, through which he overcame death; and for his rising to life again, in which we are raised to the life of your kingdom.*

This powerful and preeminent reality for the Christian is at odds with almost everything we experience in our daily life. The prevailing conviction of this world is that everything we achieve, everything we are, everything we have, comes at our own hand and through our own effort. The conviction of the gospel of Jesus Christ is the complete opposite: "It is Christ who strengthens me."

This contradiction is abundantly clear at many funerals, when the service is announced as A Service of Thanksgiving and Celebration for the Life of Mary Jones (the deceased). There is no doubt that the congregation gathers in sorrow, gathers to honor the deceased, but the Christian tradition and the liturgy we celebrate state two things most emphatically. First, death is cause for grief, but death is not the end. Death is overcome, swallowed up, in the victory of the resurrection of Christ, whose death and life have brought us new life. Second, we live our whole life, undertake its long course, knowing that we have been baptized into Christ's death and resurrection, and at the end, when our days on earth are concluded, then we know that through Christ we enter new life. But none of this is of our own doing. All of it is thanks to our Lord and Savior, Jesus Christ.

THEY SAT IN THEIR ACCUSTOMED PEW, where the family had gathered, Sunday after Sunday, just the two of them, father and son.

It would be the very last time they ever did this—sat together in church on a Sunday morning.

The gospel for the day was Luke's account of the Great Dinner.

"Come; for everything is ready now." But they all alike began to make excuses. The first said to him, "I have bought a piece of land, and I must go out and see it; please accept my regrets." Another said, "I have bought five yoke of oxen, and I am going to try them out; please accept my regrets." Another said, "I have just been married, and therefore I cannot come." So the slave returned and reported this to his master. Then the owner of the house became angry and said to his slave, "Go out at once into the streets and lanes of the town and bring the poor, the crippled, the blind, and the lame." And the slave said, "Sir, what you ordered has been done, and there is still room." Then the master said to the slave, "Go out into the roads and lanes, and compel people to come in, so that my house may be filled. For I tell you, none of those who were invited will taste my dinner."

(Luke 14:17–24)

As the son stood listening to the words of the Gospel, he became aware that the pew had started to shake, Gently, at first, then more and more vigorously, until it seemed as if the entire room was shaking.

The Gospel ended; they sat for the sermon, but the shaking continued and increased. His father was sobbing, more and more violently. The son turned to see tears streaming down his face, as he gave himself over completely to the emotion of the moment— pure and complete.

169

Neither spoke. The shaking became less and less, and finally ceased completely by the end of the sermon. When the service ended, there were fewer pleasantries and Sunday morning greetings than usual.

They drove home in silence. the father picked up the Sunday paper and walked into the living room, while the son fetched each a glass of sherry and came to sit with his father.

After he'd entered the room, he asked, "What happened?"

"What do you mean?" his father replied.

"Why were you crying?"

"It hit me. It all hit me, and I lost all control. Everything has changed since Mother died. You know that I'm not the same. Well, it's more than that." He turned and looked out the window to his right. The son waited. "More than that, far more. I've had glimpses, moments of insight, but this morning when I heard those words, those particular words, it struck me. It struck me that nothing else matters. Striving, accomplishing, working, day after day — that's not what matters, really matters, in the end. And the end is near....

"What matters from beginning to end is my relationship with God through Jesus. That's what matters. If that sounds silly or stupid, please forgive me. But after all these years, it comes down to that.

"It was your mother's death that began to open my eyes. After she left, nothing had the same brilliance. Worse than that. Most things seemed meaningless. She was the window through which I came to see everything, everything that mattered. Now she's gone. That means I have to see for myself.

"What I am beginning to see is the truth, as I've never seen it before. That's what hit me this morning, and it was more than I could stand. But I see. I really see."

HE'D KNOWN IT FOR YEARS. After all, it was why he fell in love in the first place. For some unbelievable reason, she loved him. He knew how it all began. How one thing led to another over several years, but it was still a miracle, and it made no sense.

She loved him. She really did, and for no reason that made any sense to him. After all, what was lovable? Not much, if anything, only it was true. She loved him. And that made all the difference.

It made more difference than any other single thing. It was why he got up in the morning and why he went to bed at night, in her embrace, to wake again and give thanks for one more day. One more day.

Oh, there was more. The getting and spending, the doing and the thinking, the running and the walking, the chasing after dreams. They were even important. But what made them important came from one source—her love, her being, her presence. That was a miracle. None of it made sense. It was not even rational. But it was the central and most important event and reality of his life. A miracle, a miracle that could only have happened, could only be real because of the presence and person of Jesus Christ.

Where do we go from here?

Grant us the gift of your Spirit, that we may know Christ and make him known; and through him, at all times and in all places, may give thanks to you in all things. Amen. It was John Kennedy, who wisely said in his inaugural address, "On this earth, God's work must surely be our own." Jesus has neither hands, nor feet, nor voice, nor opportunity to be present in this world save through who we — you and I — are and what we do on this earth, where God's work must surely be our own.

That which we do, we do through Christ and in Christ's name. God's Holy Spirit is visited upon us for this purpose. Jesus said that God would send the Comforter to be among us and for us and with us until he comes again in power and great glory. So it is that we pray: *Grant us the gift of your Spirit, that we may know Christ and make him known; and through him, at all times and in all places, may give thanks to you in all things.*

Grace is a gift that is completely undeserved and unexpected. Grace comes from outside, beyond a person. Grace is the presence of God breaking into our life when least expected. No one has ever seen God but everyone has received grace.

Anne. Her name means grace, and I knew that, I just knew, almost from the very beginning. Anne had never happened to me before and will never happen again. Good or bad, each day spent with Anne is greeted with hope. Every day is not smooth. Some have been unwelcome, marked by death, disappointment, serious illness, and loss.

The most memorable days have been most challenging, days when we cried, days that brought depth and strength, refashioning the love that draws and holds us together.

One of these days happened in March. We were driving home from a sabbatical in Santa Fe. Early in the morning, as we crossed from Florida into Georgia, a fierce pain struck my forehead, threatening to split it open. As I slumped in the passenger seat, scarcely able to see, out of nowhere loomed a blue sign with a large H. We followed more signs to the hospital in Thomasville. A wheelchair appeared; someone rolled me into the emergency room, helped me onto a gurney, left us alone, and summoned a doctor.

Neither one of us said the words we were thinking, that we were convinced the end was near. Anne fished in my coat pocket and produced the well-worn seventeenth-century silver crucifix she had given me. "Here," she said, "here, hold this," as she wrapped her hands around mine, and, together, we grasped the cross for dear life.

"I love you," she said. The words were life-saving. "I love you, too." Silence. Our marriage might be coming to an end, but now that we had pledged our love in the presence of the cross, what else was there?

Singular moments, unexpected, mark each life. They linger, keeping the long ago alive and making it possible for the present to reinvent itself. "Pay attention," Anne often says. "Pay attention to what you've been given. Every moment is a gift."

God dwells in each moment. Each is a gift. Each is marked by prayer. Prayer is the presence of God.